Wilhelmina Barns-Graham

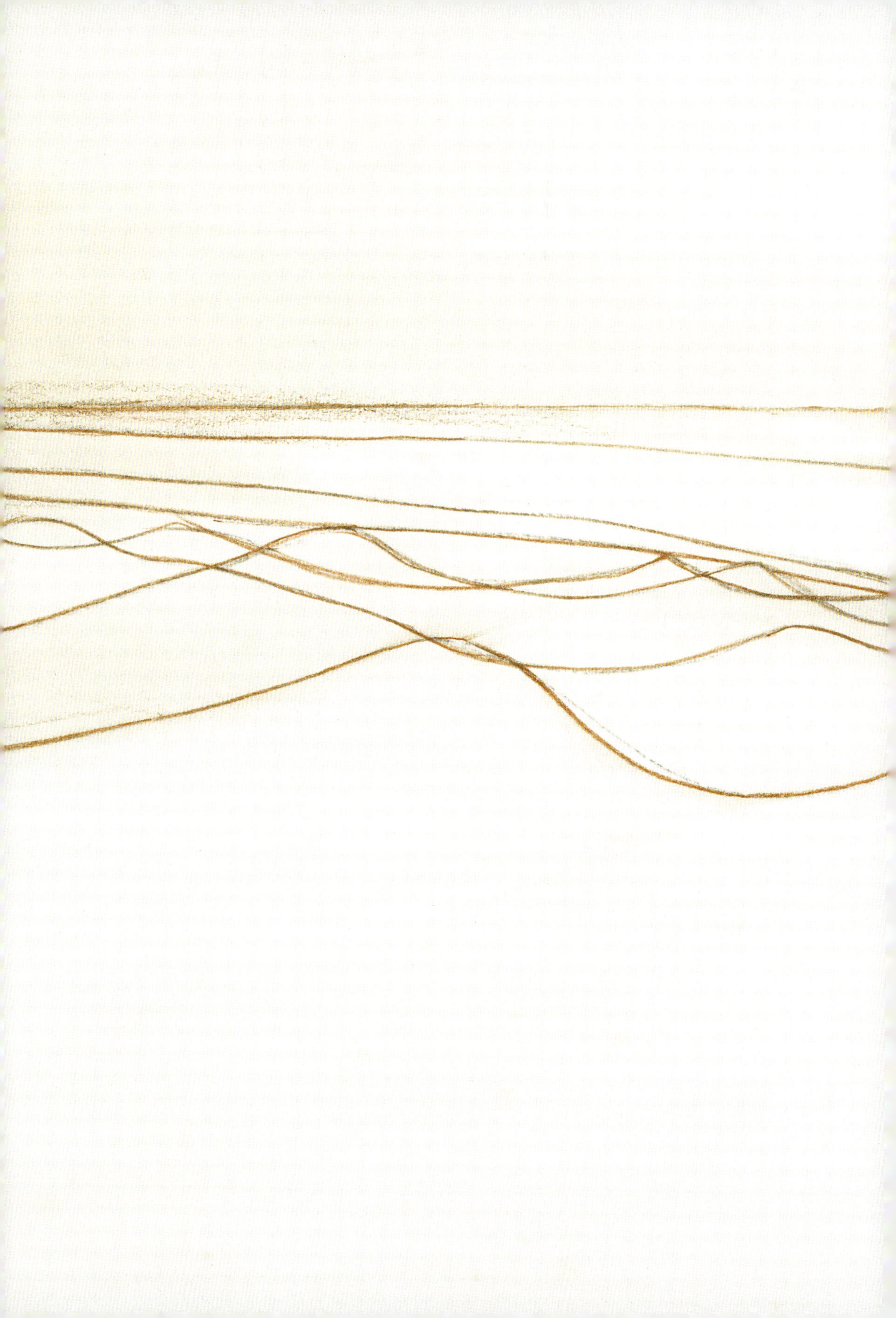

Wilhelmina Barns-Graham

Virginia Button

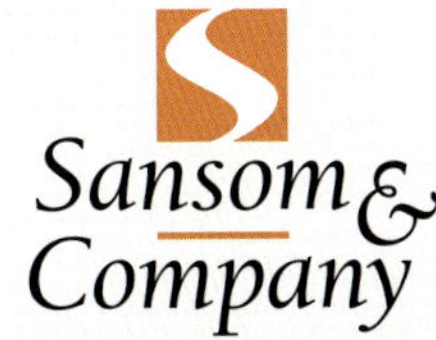

Sansom & Company

Reprinted 2023 · first published in 2020 by Sansom and Company,
a publishing imprint of Redcliffe Press Ltd.,
81G Pembroke Road, Bristol BS8 3EA
www.sansomandcompany.co.uk · info@sansomandcompany.co.uk

ISBN 978-1-911408-64-2

British Library Cataloguing-in-Publication Data
A catalogue record for this book is available from the British Library.

Design and typesetting by E&P Design

Printed and bound by Akcent Media

Frontispiece · *Eight Lines, Porthmeor* · 1986

Contents

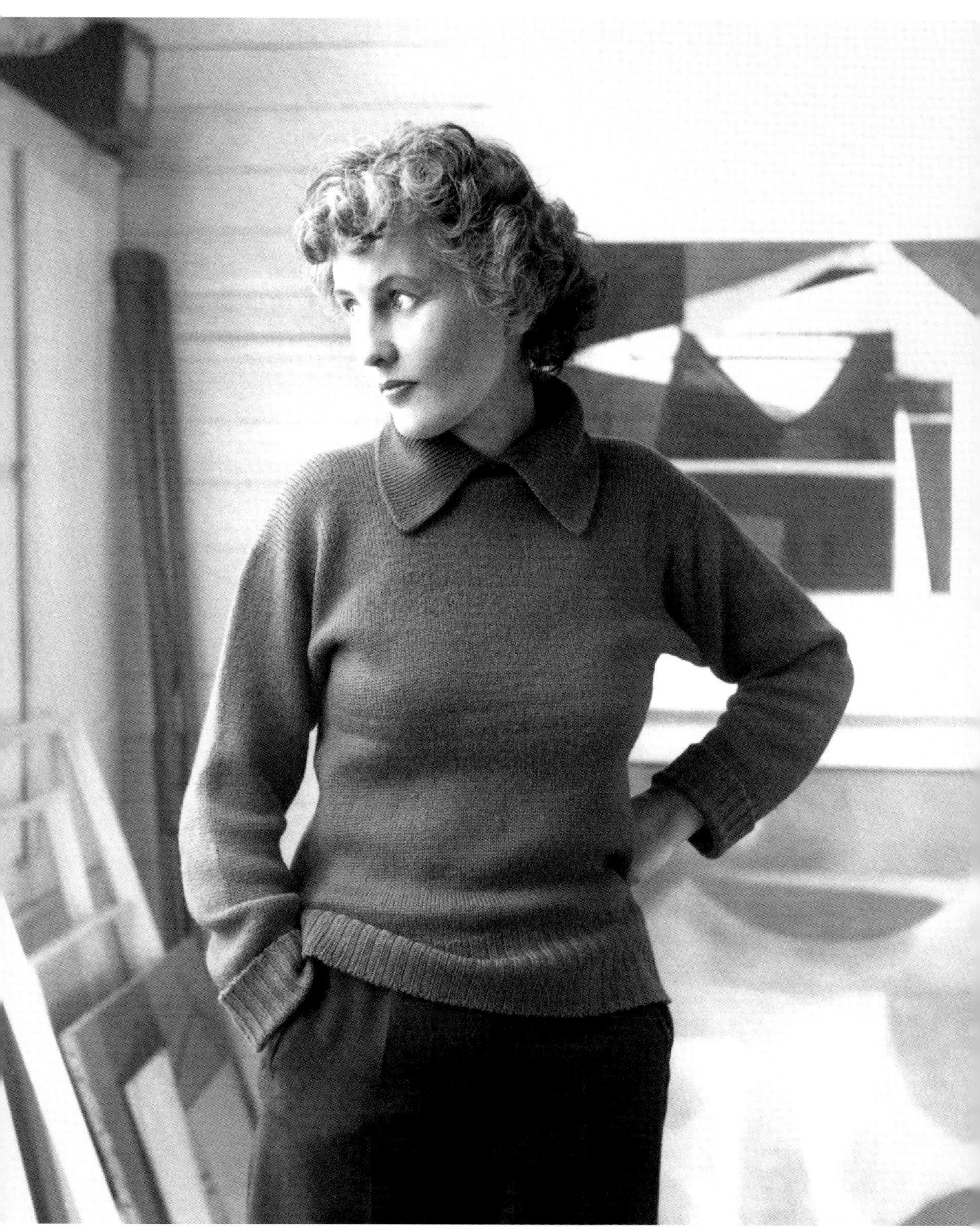

Barns-Graham in her Porthmeor Studio, 1955

photo Adrian Flowers/Adrian Flowers Archive

1 Introduction

Born in St Andrews, Scotland, Wilhelmina Barns-Graham (1912–2004) was a core member of the group of modern artists that coalesced around St Ives in Cornwall between the 1940s and 1960s. In the aftermath of the Second World War they sought in different ways to make meaning of the world through an art of renewal — broadly speaking a nature-based abstraction — and in doing so gained international critical attention.

Despite a disciplined, single-minded commitment to a painter's life over seven decades, Barns-Graham's reputation as a painter has rested largely on a group of works produced in the context of 'St Ives' in the late 1940s and in the early 1950s following a trip to the Grindelwald Glacier in Switzerland. In the febrile, competitive atmosphere of the post-war art world, she was feted in the 1950s as Britain's leading woman abstract painter. But for various reasons, by the early 1960s she had fallen from grace.

As a younger woman she had overcome a series of challenges, not least an overbearing father who opposed his daughter's pursuit of 'this art nonsense'.[1] She also battled with chronic and debilitating respiratory illnesses, but such obstacles served to strengthen her commitment to her vocation. She earned the respect and support of her tutors at Edinburgh College of Art (ECA) and senior artists such as Ben Nicholson (1894–1982) and Bernard Leach (1887–1979). But a crisis in her personal life in the late 1950s, and the shifting cultural landscape — including the eclipse of 'St Ives' as an internationally recognised locus of the avant-garde — left her feeling isolated, in her own words a 'lone wolf'.[2] In mid-career she pursued the objective discipline of a mathematically-based abstraction, but remained ambivalent towards an art devoid of feeling.[3] Having reached an impasse in the 1980s (then in her seventies), she experienced

a breakthrough, and right up to her death aged ninety-one she delighted
in a period of heightened creativity, released from any anxiety of influence or
expectation. During this late phase she enjoyed the support of devoted friends
and admirers alongside increasing institutional recognition of her achievement.

The non-linear trajectory of Barns-Graham's career and the diversity of her
output have made her difficult to sum up. She has been hard to classify, often
falling between groups or categories. Although a key member of 'St Ives', her
contribution – or place in its story – has been overlooked until relatively recently.
Her first retrospective exhibition in 1989 was accompanied by an insightful
appraisal by Douglas Hall, followed in 2001 by Lynne Green's authoritative,
comprehensive monograph *W. Barns-Graham: A Studio Life* (revised 2011)
and this book owes a debt to their primary researches.

Barns-Graham clearly felt that as a woman she had been unfairly side-lined
from the history of 'St Ives', both in the 1950s and later when it was reassessed
by the Tate Gallery's landmark exhibition of 1985, 'St Ives, 1939–64: Twenty Five
Years of Painting, Sculpture and Pottery'. Tate St Ives subsequently explored her
work in two solo exhibitions, but her position in the 'St Ives' story has remained
peripheral, for example, in Chris Stephens' recent definitive study *St Ives: The
Art and the Artists* (2018) she plays only a marginal role.[4] Perhaps this is hardly
surprising in a narrative with a strong cast of male leads operating in a competitive field. Following the relative relaxation of gender roles during the
war years, the post-war years were characterised by a resurgent masculinity
and this was played out in the chauvinistic milieu of 'St Ives'.[5] Any overview
of Barns-Graham's life and work needs to consider this context, in which she
was both supported by such 'father' figures as Nicholson but also dismissed
as his follower, and despite appearances, not fully accepted by her male peers.[6]

Her awareness of gender-bias is suggested by the pleasure she took in the
ambiguity of her own name: known as 'Willie', and often only by the initial
of her first name, she could easily be mistaken for a man. Her future husband,
the South African poet and writer David Lewis (b.1922), recalled his surprise
on meeting her in summer 1948 at Nicholson's home in Carbis Bay:

> *At the time she was painting a series of street scenes of houses with steps
> and balustrades, and was known as W. Balustrade Graham. I was surprised
> to find that 'Balustrade' was not a man but a woman, and a beautiful
> woman at that, with blue eyes that flashed like knives.*[7]

Later in life Barns-Graham confessed that she had herself been prejudiced
against women artists, believing that only a very few would be any good, as

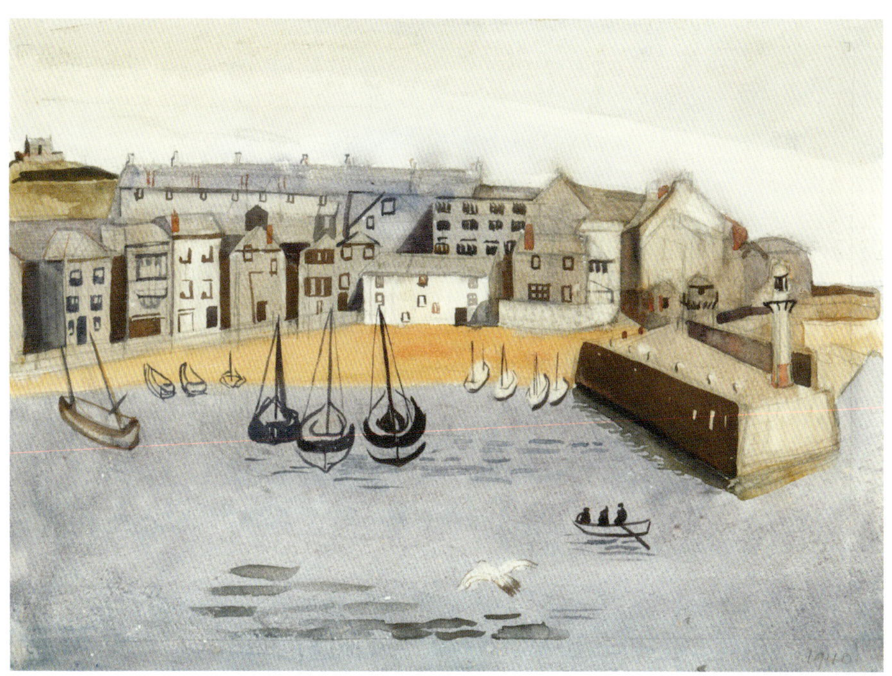

St Ives Harbour · 1940 · gouache on paper · 29 x 39 cm BGT6403

she told Susan Loppert in 1996: 'There are plenty of women painting but (I had a little of that chauvinist attitude myself) how many really interesting creative women artists are there?'[8] With the exception of Barbara Hepworth (1903–1975) who forged a starry, international career, making an impact as a modern artist in the mid-twentieth century and being a woman were largely incompatible. Calling out discrimination didn't help her cause, as implied by Michael Bird in his comparison of Barns-Graham's confrontational response to sexism with the complicit approach taken by Sandra Blow (1925–2006), who spent a year in St Ives in 1957 and enjoyed commercial success in the late 1950s:

> *Unlike Barns-Graham, who into her nineties was still to be heard complaining volubly about male artists' conspiracy to keep women down, Blow saw the British art world's unwritten social code as a game that could be played effectively once you knew the rules.*[9]

There were of course other factors that affected her career, not least differing views on the nature of abstract art. Throughout her life she produced representational images alongside abstract paintings, which cast doubt on her purpose and radicalism. However, in the post-war period a number of artists including Hepworth and Nicholson adopted this middle ground, a position endorsed by influential art historian and critic Herbert Read (1893–1968) in *The Meaning of Art* (1931, reprinted 1951):

*But the changeover from one style to another, from realism to abstraction
and from abstraction to realism, need not be accompanied by any deep
psychological process. It is merely a change of direction, of destination.
What is constant is the desire to create a reality, a coherent world of
vital images.*[10]

Read's analysis provides a useful way of understanding the variety in Barns-
Graham's oeuvre. He was briefly Professor of Fine Art at Edinburgh University
in the early 1930s and as a student at ECA she attended his lectures, which
formed the basis of *The Meaning of Art*. She owned a hardback copy printed
in 1932 and a paperback edition of 1951, which she marked-up heavily. Read
became a towering figure in the British art world (with strong connections
to 'St Ives'), but would himself be accused of eclecticism in his support for
competing styles of art. Similarly, the apparent diversity of Barns-Graham's
work — her attachment to both realism and abstraction — made it both easy
to view her output as lacking direction and difficult to identify her signature
style. She also liked to work in series to explore an idea, sometimes over years,
and often returned to earlier themes.[11] Versatile and receptive to new influences
she worked in different styles, motivated primarily by a desire to 'express *feeling*
and transmit *understanding*'.[12] The idea that creative integrity depended on a
responsive artistic sensibility rather than on style was articulated by Read in
Art Now (1933):

*It is true, of course, that the original sensibility of the artist is not static or
inelastic; it adjusts its pitch, like a voice, to its environment. A genuine artist
may, in the length of his life, so change his style that the individual unity of
his work may be in doubt — there is little similarity between the early and
the late paintings of Cézanne.*[13]

In providing an introduction to the artist, this book begins with an overview
of her life and work, with subsequent chapters focusing on key aspects of
her art. Chapter Two considers her first mature statement as an artist in the
context of 'St Ives' in the immediate post-war period. At this time the theories
of the Scottish polymath and natural scientist D'Arcy Wentworth Thompson
(1860–1948) transformed her understanding of nature and its processes.
At heart she was a romantic artist, for whom nature was a source of endless
fascination and wonder, a sentiment poignantly expressed in her statement
about drawing of 1992:

*Being in the presence of the power and awe of nature, be it to study the
effect of glaciers in Switzerland, the rain on clay formations in Tuscany, the
lava forms and disturbances in the volcanic areas of Lanzarote, to the passing*

cloud shadows on the hills and sea of Orkney, or the wind movements on sand in Fife, all wonders emphasising the realisation of the importance of being at one with nature. This is a contemplation of sensing out, feeling and understanding particular rhythms not just on the surface but underground as in Cornwall.[14]

The distinctive, architectural quality of Barns-Graham's drawing or 'line' was admired throughout her career. She constantly returned to drawing as a way of translating her inner perception of the external, natural world. Chapter Three discusses the significance of drawing to her painting and her artistic identity.

St Ives was her home from 1940 to the end of her life, though after 1960, when she inherited property near St Andrews, she spent winters in Fife. Green has drawn attention to the artist's Scottish identity and evidenced her artistic credentials prior to arriving in St Ives.[15] The final chapter considers colour's central role in Barns-Graham's work, from the early influence of the Scottish Colourists, through explorations of colour theory in the 1960s and 1970s, to the vibrant paintings and silkscreen prints of her last decades. While continuing to use proportional structures the late works represent a relaxation of constraints, finally celebrating her very personal perceptions as a synesthetic, in which objects such as words, letters and shapes are linked to colour and emotions.[16]

In the face of a turbulent and rapidly changing world, personal disappointments and challenges, Barns-Graham embraced constant flux, as seen in the forces and patterns of nature itself, which she explored incessantly using different strategies across media. Her pursuit of the possible relationship of painting to human perception and experience culminated in an efflorescence of life-affirming works, in which she finally found her voice.

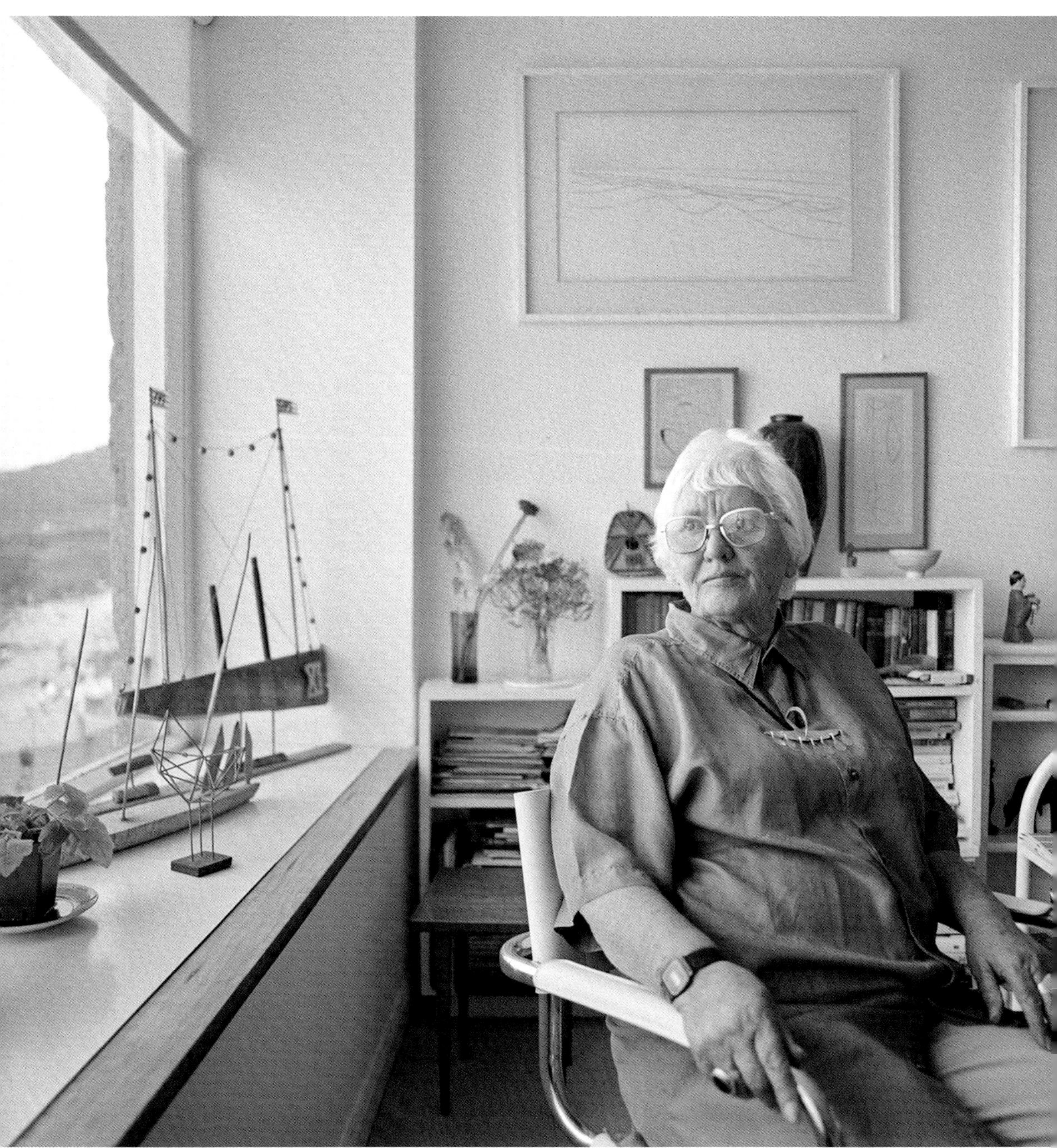

Barns-Graham in her Barnaloft sitting room overlooking Porthmeor Beach, St Ives, 1993
photo © Anne-Katrin Purkiss

2 **Life and Work**
an overview

Through keen observation and experimentation, and informed by other disciplines – geometry, science and philosophy, as well as art – Wilhelmina Barns-Graham pursued her own perceptions of the world through painting, drawing, reliefs and printmaking. She worked through thematic ideas in series, but she was never programmatic, never really closing down an idea. For her there was always more to explore.

The amount and variety of her output over an exceptionally long career has made her work difficult to define; however, her search for meaning was consistently rooted in her love of nature, particularly its hidden structures and constantly changing elemental forces. Nature remained a touchstone. Accessed through an immersive, intuitive approach to drawing, it continued to be a subject and source of renewal, even when her work relinquished obvious reference to the external world.

As a woman artist, Barns-Graham occupied a unique position in the narrative of 'St Ives' modernism. Over the years, and while others departed, St Ives remained her home. The story of her life and career is bound up with 'St Ives' and how she absorbed its ideas and influences and grappled with its internal machinations and rivalries to forge her own path.

Arriving in St Ives in 1940 shortly after Ben Nicholson, Barbara Hepworth and Naum Gabo (1890–1977), she became part of their avant-garde circle and recognised as an abstract artist in her own right. When 'St Ives' modernism was in the ascendant during the 1950s she was one of its rising stars; as a woman artist her reputation was second only to Hepworth's. But for various reasons she felt increasingly overlooked by her male colleagues.

In the early 1960s, as the nature-based abstraction associated with 'St Ives' gave way to new agendas, Barns-Graham changed tack towards a more geometrical, systems-based approach to painting that lasted for over 20 years. This has made her career appear disjointed, and much writing about the artist since the 1990s has set out to evidence the continuity of themes and interests underpinning her work.[1] This dramatic shift occurred as she turned 50 and, though partly a response to changing trends in art, it was inextricably linked to a mid-life crisis. Distressed by the failure of her marriage and feeling marginalised by the masculine culture of 'St Ives', she withdrew from the pack and determined to make a fresh start. Despite her continued dedication to her vocation as an artist, critical appreciation eluded her until the mid-1980s. Happily, this late phase marked the beginning of a reconciliation of the different aspects of her work, and a sense of real achievement.

Her fortunes as an artist were undoubtedly affected by strong male influences, which she had to negotiate. For example, her friendship with Nicholson, 18 years her senior and an important mentor and a supporter of her work, cast her in the role of his follower. For many years in St Ives, Barns-Graham was virtually the only woman working within a peer group of ambitious male artists, and she took pride in being, as she thought, 'one of the boys'.[2] She later discovered with some bitterness that — in the context of the macho 1950s — she wasn't taken as seriously. This was in contrast to Hepworth. Despite intimating that 'we women should stick together', Hepworth's own need for recognition in a male dominated world, in which she herself was positioned as pupil to Henry Moore's (1898–1986) 'master', left little room for sisterly altruism.[3] For young men returning from active service at the end of the Second World War, such as the working-class 'St Ives' artist Terry Frost (1915–2003), art and bohemianism provided sanctuary and the promise of a better life. For Barns-Graham, it offered sanctuary of a different kind; escape from an authoritarian father, and freedom as a woman to live independently and explore her creative impulses.

Pursuing an artist's life: early years in Scotland
Barns-Graham was born in St Andrews, Fife, on 8 June 1912, the eldest of three children to Allan Barns-Graham and his wife Wilhelmina (née Bayne Meldrum). By all accounts her upbringing was austere, religious and patriarchal. Her father was a 'laird', comfortably off though not wealthy, a respected philanthropist in the community but a bullying father at home. To escape her old-fashioned, landed-gentry background and establish herself as a professional artist required considerable determination. She later recalled her childhood ambition and predilection for abstraction:

I was eight years old when I knew I wanted to be an artist. Amongst my earliest memories are my pencil and crayon drawings, abstract irregular or rectangular shapes, usually outlined in blue and filled with a single colour. These were very private, like secret rooms ... In later childhood, using a compass, I made many abstract pencil designs. In my teens I discovered Cézanne and have admired his well-structured 'architectural' paintings ever since.[4]

She first encountered Paul Cézanne's (1839–1906) work in 1930 as an 18 year old in Paris with her aunt, Mary Niesh, who often played the role of 'guardian angel' to her niece. Barns-Graham's parents opposed her desire to study art and in 1931 enrolled her on a course at Edinburgh College of Domestic Science. After six, miserable months Mary offered financial support enabling her to study at Edinburgh College of Art (ECA) for one year, with subsequent study dependent on scholarships. Her father conceded, though he remained disapproving of his daughter's career until she left Scotland in 1940.[5] She later reflected that considering her physical frailty her father's hostility towards her insecure and challenging life choice might have been partly justified.[6]

Barns-Graham suffered throughout her life with severe respiratory conditions, especially when under stress. During her twenties, uncertainty around the continuation of her studies provoked prolonged bouts of illness that interrupted her enrolment at ECA, which lasted until 1937. Annual scholarships from 1935 enabled her to continue intermittently with postgraduate study until 1940. This unusually long apprenticeship meant that when she arrived in St Ives to complete her final scholarship aged 27, she was well prepared to embark on her career, with knowledge of art history, modern art and hours of studio practice under her belt. Photos of her diploma show in 1937 confirm that she was an accomplished practitioner of traditional fine art skills. The general course at ECA trained students in the discipline of eye-hand co-ordination, especially through drawing, to help them see and appreciate beauty in nature. This discipline provided a lasting foundation for Barns-Graham, enhancing her ability to capture the essence of a subject.[7]

Lynne Green's research into the artist's formative years has countered the view that Barns-Graham was a blank canvas before her association with 'St Ives'. At ECA, run by Hubert Wellington (1879–1967), she was taught by some of Scotland's leading artists, including the 'Scottish Colourist' S.J. Peploe (1871–1935) and William Gillies (1898–1973), who promoted the importance of craft. Barns-Graham also admired John Maxwell (1905–1962), who painted landscapes and imaginative subjects influenced by Paul Klee (1879–1940) and Joan Miró (1893–1983).[8] Her fellow students included William Gear (1915–1997) and Margaret Mellis (1914–2009), who both became great friends of the artist.

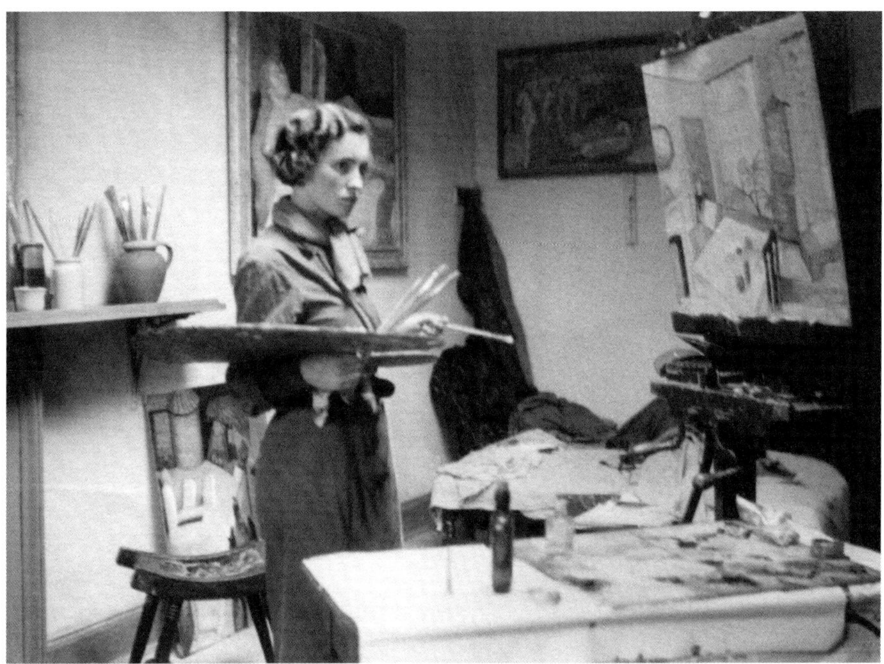

Barns-Graham in her Alva Street Studio, Edinburgh, painting *Edinburgh Interior*, 1937

Mellis married the art critic and painter Adrian Stokes (1902–1972) in 1938, moving to Carbis Bay near St Ives, which influenced Barns-Graham's decision to go there. In the 1930s Barns-Graham also became a friend of the painters Robert Colquhoun (1914–1962) and Robert MacBryde (1913–1966), then students in Glasgow, remaining in touch with them after their move to London in 1941.

In Edinburgh the Scottish Society of Artists provided access to exhibitions of modern and contemporary art, showing, for example, paintings by Ben and Winifred Nicholson (1893–1981) in 1931 and in 1937 hosting 'Constructive Art', a group show including work by Nicholson, Hepworth and Moore ahead of the publication of *Circle: International Survey of Constructive Art*. That Barns-Graham acquired a copy of *Circle* in 1937 indicates her interest in abstraction, though there was little context for such radicalism at ECA.[9] In the late 1930s, she explored modern approaches to painting, as evidenced by *Edinburgh Interior* (above and right) with its Matisse-like compression of space and bright hues, and *The Episcopal Church, Aviemore* (p. 18) which comprises simplified, inter-locking shapes in a style learnt from Gillies and Maxwell, while the theme resonates with Christopher Wood's (1901–1930) naïve Breton churches of the 1920s.

In summer 1938 she was forced to postpone a six-month travelling scholar-ship to Europe due to ill-health, and the outbreak of the Second World War

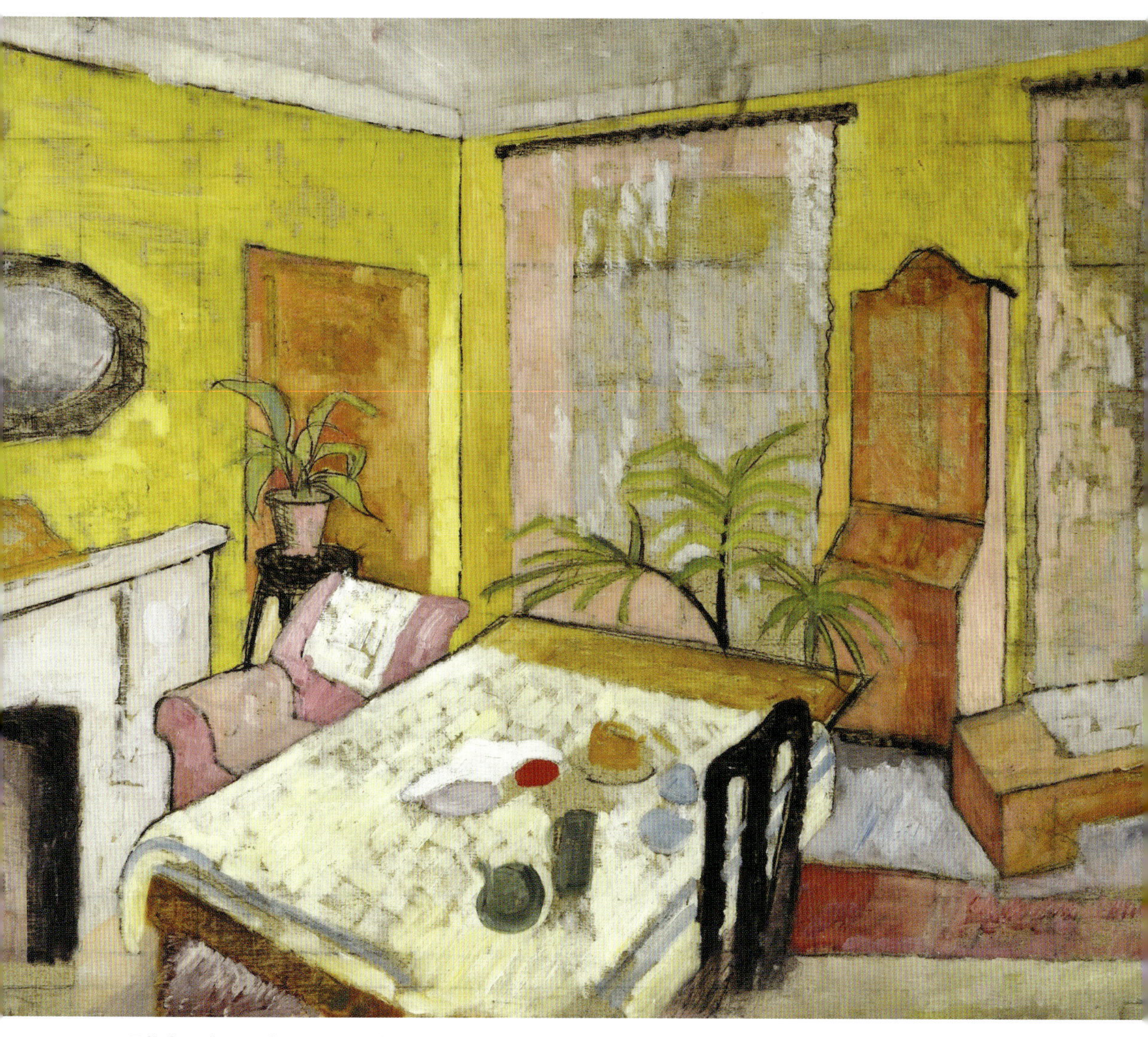

Edinburgh Interior · 1937 · oil on hardboard · 60.5 x 76 cm

in September 1939 put a final stop to this, but thanks to Wellington's interven-
tion she was able to complete her studies in the art colony of St Ives. He knew
like-minded artists would be there, namely, Stokes and Mellis and their friends,
including Nicholson and Hepworth, who moved to Carbis Bay shortly before
the outbreak of war, and Russian Constructivist émigré Naum Gabo and his wife
the painter Miriam Israels, who had followed them there from London. While
there would be restrictions on her practice — painting and drawing subjects
outside was illegal during wartime — it was agreed that Cornwall would be safe

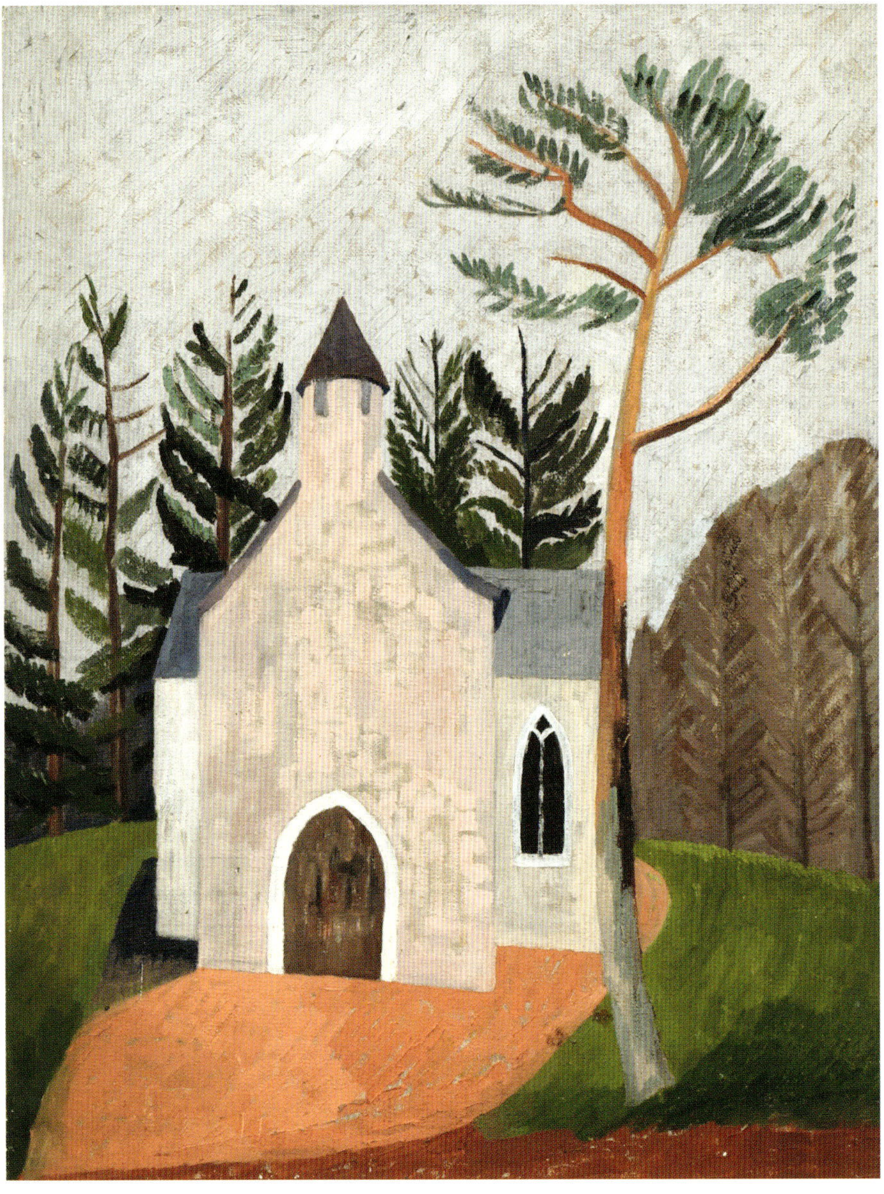

The Episcopal Church, Aviemore · 1938 · oil on wood panel · 61 x 46.8 cm BGT1892

from falling bombs, and good for her health.[10] Importantly for Barns-Graham, the move to the tiny fishing town in March 1940 represented independence from her family and the beginning of a love affair with Cornwall that would last for over 60 years.

'St Ives' 1940s: friends and factions

'St Ives' modernism, or the 'St Ives School', was not an organised group, but a shifting set of relationships between artists, who over a period stretching from the late 1930s to the mid-1960s shared similar aims and sources, and were recognised for their internationally significant contribution to modern art. Embedded in the avant-garde community from the outset, Barns-Graham established herself as an equal within a generation of talented male artists. But during this period she was particularly affected by the divisions that arose within the tightly-knit, fractious art community, when tensions between opposing factions — initially between the traditionalists and the moderns and then within the modernist circle itself — came to a head.

As England's leading abstract artists, Nicholson and Hepworth were deeply committed to establishing a centre for advanced practice based on pre-war constructivist abstraction. Their influence on the younger generation was considerable, reflecting their professionalism and intense dedication to their work. Gabo also exerted a powerful influence, and — along with a number of her peers, notably her close friend John Wells (1907–2000) and Peter Lanyon (1918–1964) — Barns-Graham was profoundly affected by the work and ideas of the Russian artist, although he departed from Cornwall in 1946.

She was also involved with the established art colony through membership of the St Ives Society of Artists and the Newlyn Society of Artists from 1942, and through her friendship with the highly respected, marine landscape painter Robert Borlase Smart (1881–1947). Within a fortnight of her arrival in St Ives he had found her a space in the Atlantic-facing Porthmeor Studios. Borlase Smart set out to 'like the best in both traditional and advanced art' and Barns-Graham acted as a conduit, introducing him to the recently relocated 'moderns' Nicholson and Hepworth.[11] He attempted to rejuvenate the art colony by bringing traditionalist and avant-garde artists together in the St Ives Society of Artists — a plan that spectacularly backfired following his death in 1947. But like Borlase Smart, her first mentor in St Ives, Barns-Graham was eager to get along with everyone.

In the war years she contributed as best she could to the war effort, volunteering as a factory worker making camouflage nets, and then becoming an air raid warden. These years might be seen as an extension of Barns-Graham's studies, as she collected ideas for future work in her notebooks and explored a variety of subjects in different styles, including Alfred Wallis-type coastal views such as *Island Sheds, St Ives No. 1* (right). She was acquainted with Wallis (1855–1942) and, like other 'St Ives' artists, learnt from him that depiction of a subject involved memory and experience as much as looking. Two contrasting works of 1945 – *Froth and Seaweed* (below) loosely painted on card and the tightly composed, grid-like *Studio Interior (Red Stool, Studio)* (p. 22) – also show her experimenting with abstract forms. The latter, with its orderly representation of her studio containing three blank canvases, might be viewed as a manifesto of intent, the yellow jug representing the artist, poised to make her mark.[12]

In 1945 Lanyon returned from service and the presence of the pre-war avant-garde also began to attract artists to Cornwall, either for extended visits or to relocate, as Wynter and Frost did in 1946. This was an exciting and stimulating period, as the community of aspiring young artists expanded. Lanyon was instrumental in setting up the 'Crypt Group', a gathering of exclusively modern but diverse younger artists, who – dissatisfied with their allocated space in the St Ives Society of Artists exhibitions at the Mariner's Church – held a series of shows between 1946 and 1948 in the crypt beneath it. Barns-Graham took part in the second and third of these exhibitions, in 1947 and 1948. A frequently reproduced Central Office of Information (COI) photograph documents those

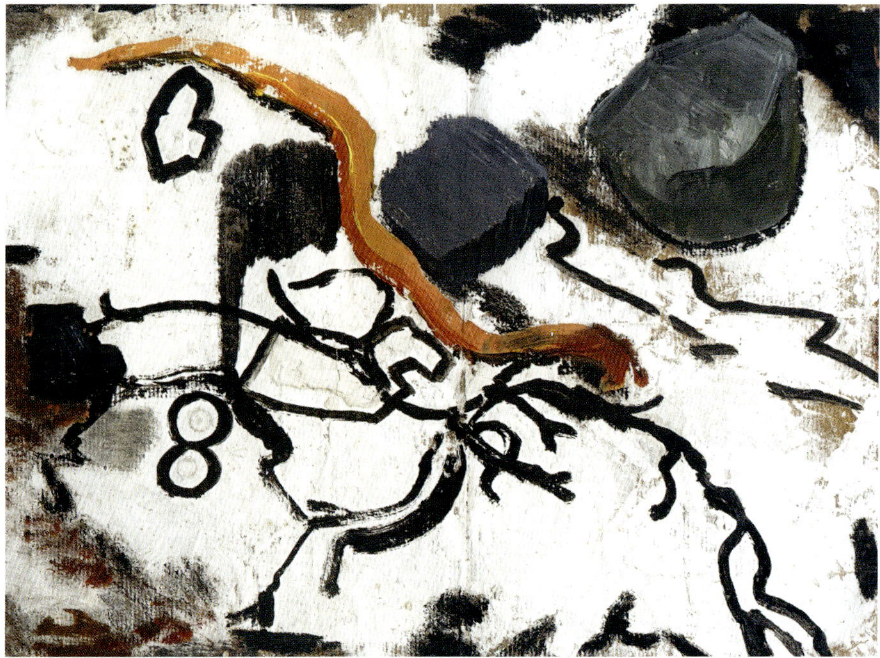

Froth and Seaweed · 1945 · oil on paper · 26.8 x 37.8 cm BGT1082

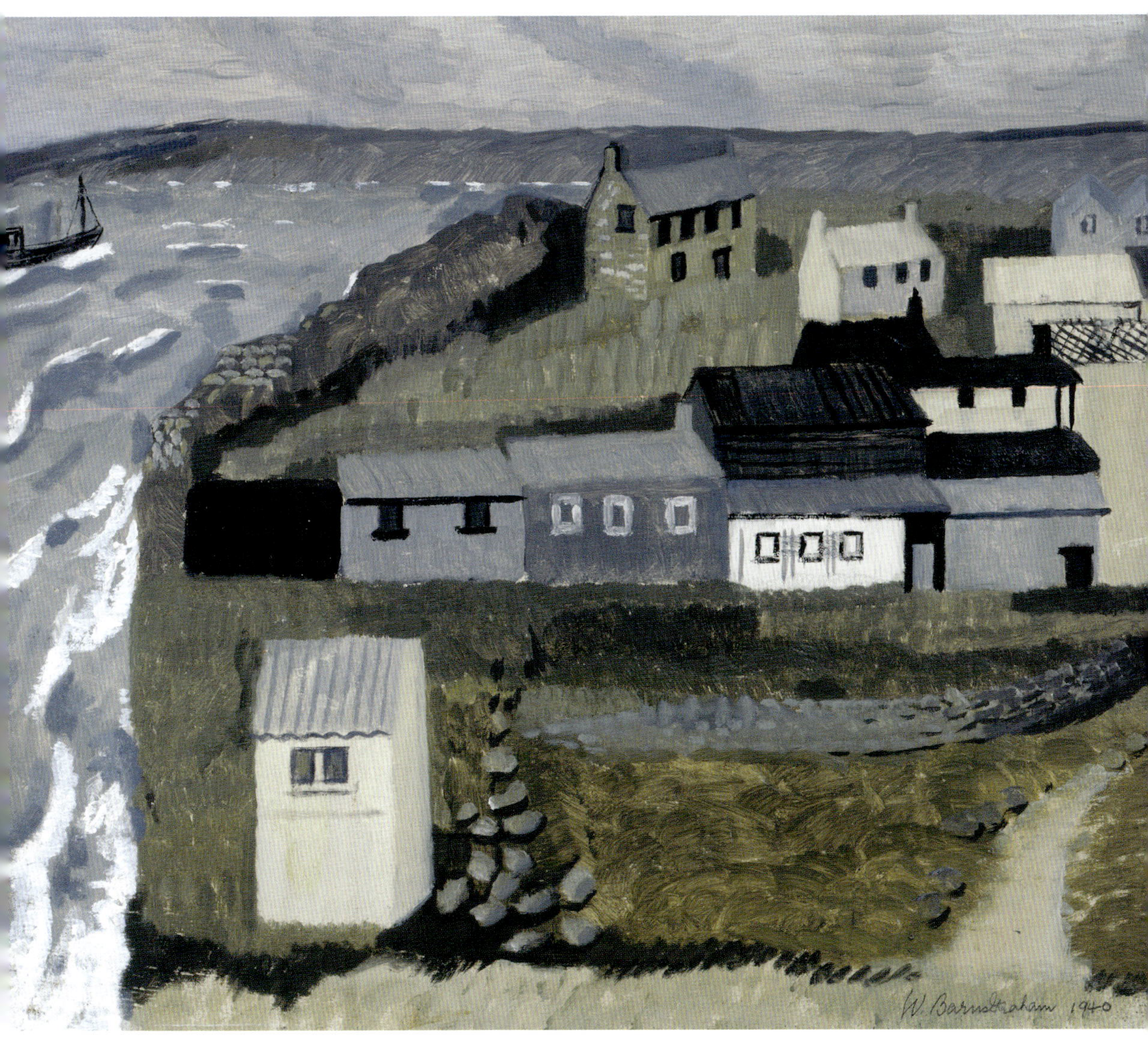

Island Sheds, St Ives No. 1 · 1940 · oil on plywood · 33 x 40.5 cm

Tate · presented by the artist 1999 · T07546 · photo © Tate

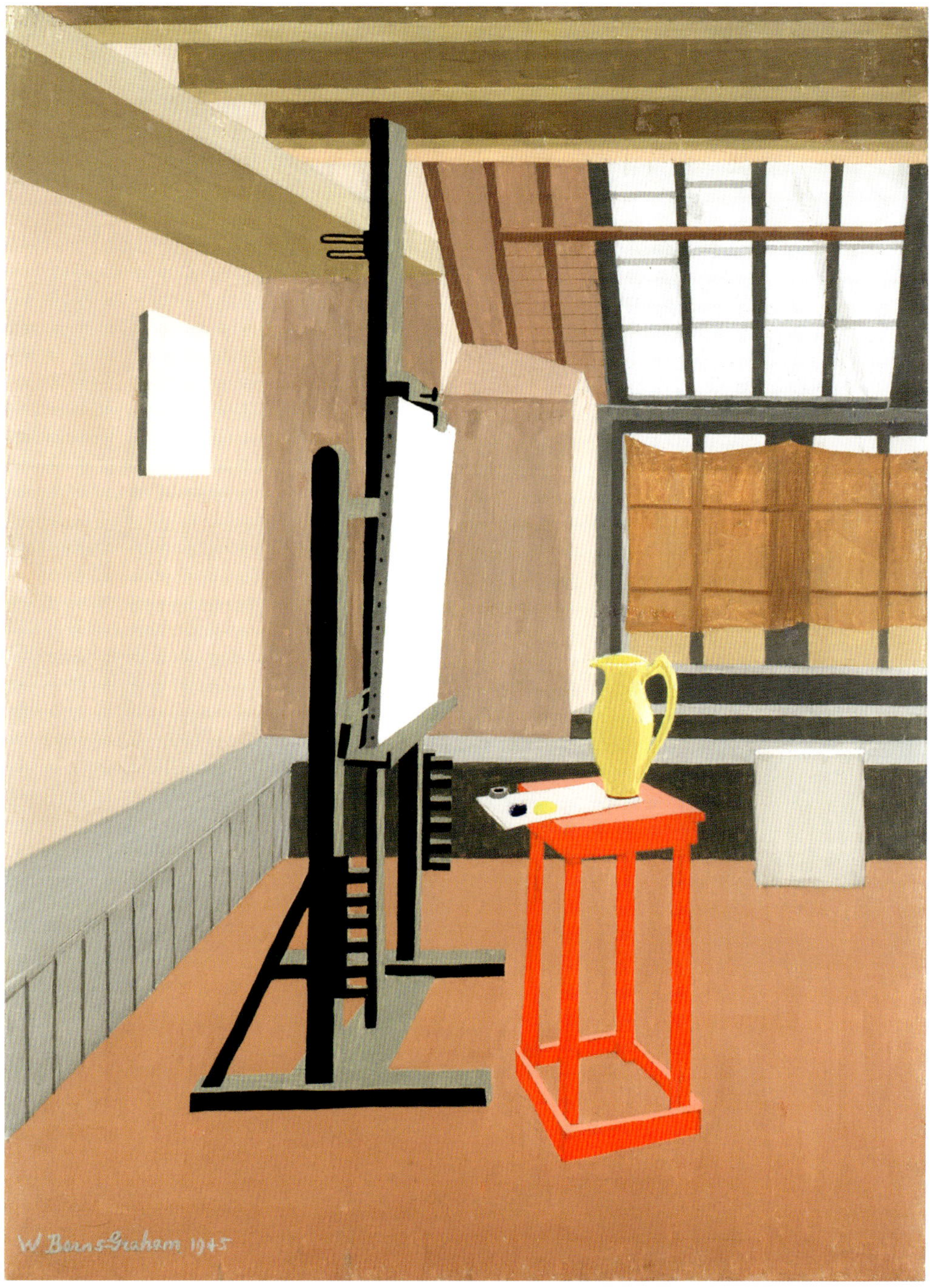

Studio Interior (Red Stool, Studio) · 1945 · oil on canvas · 60 x 45.6 cm

BGT6408

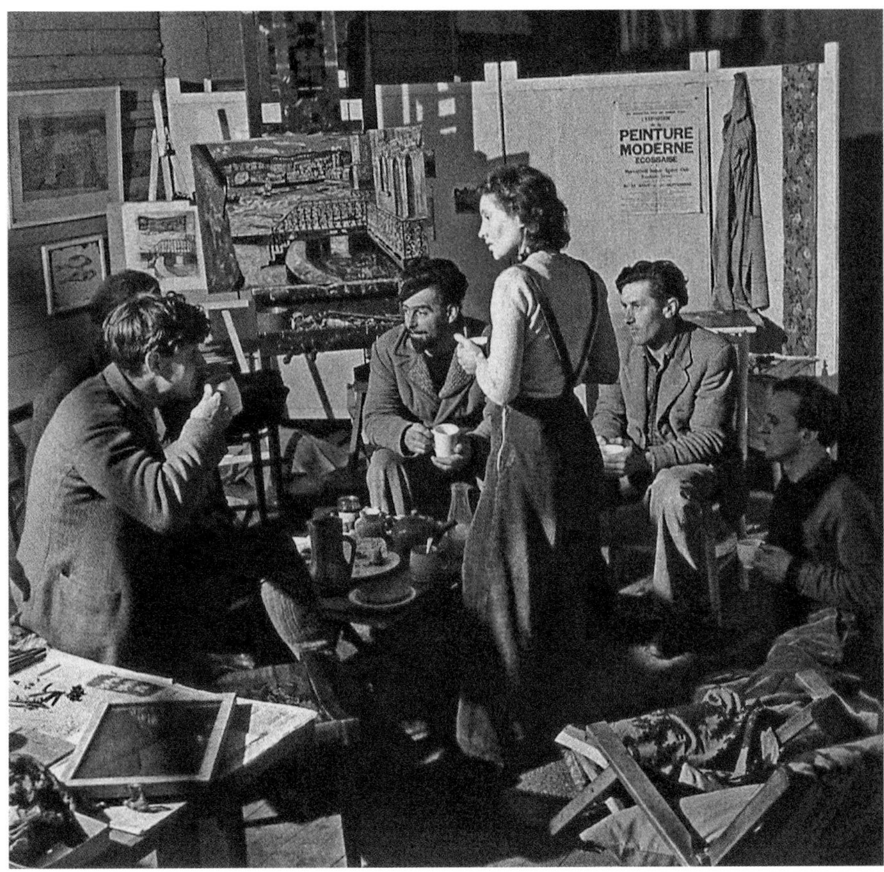

A meeting of the Crypt Group, 1947. Left to right: Peter Lanyon, Bryan Wynter (hidden), Sven Berlin, Barns-Graham, John Wells and Guido Morris

involved in the second show meeting in her studio (above). Although the artists participating varied and there was no group identity or manifesto, they nonetheless attracted attention and Lanyon had ambitions to present the group in London. Barns-Graham's absence from the first Crypt Group show (she was on an annual visit to her family, and apparently not approached to participate) served to marginalise her in subsequent accounts of the development of 'St Ives'.[13]

In the later 1940s she was drawn increasingly to architectural and gritty sub-jects, such as the rubbish dump, in marked contrast to the picturesque views favoured by more traditional artists and the tourist market. A notable example is *Box Factory Fire* (overleaf), shown in the Crypt exhibition that year, in which the flame-ravaged contents of the building nestle as if alive within its exterior

overleaf · **Box Factory Fire** · 1948 · oil on canvas · 55.8 x 76.2 cm · BGT6216

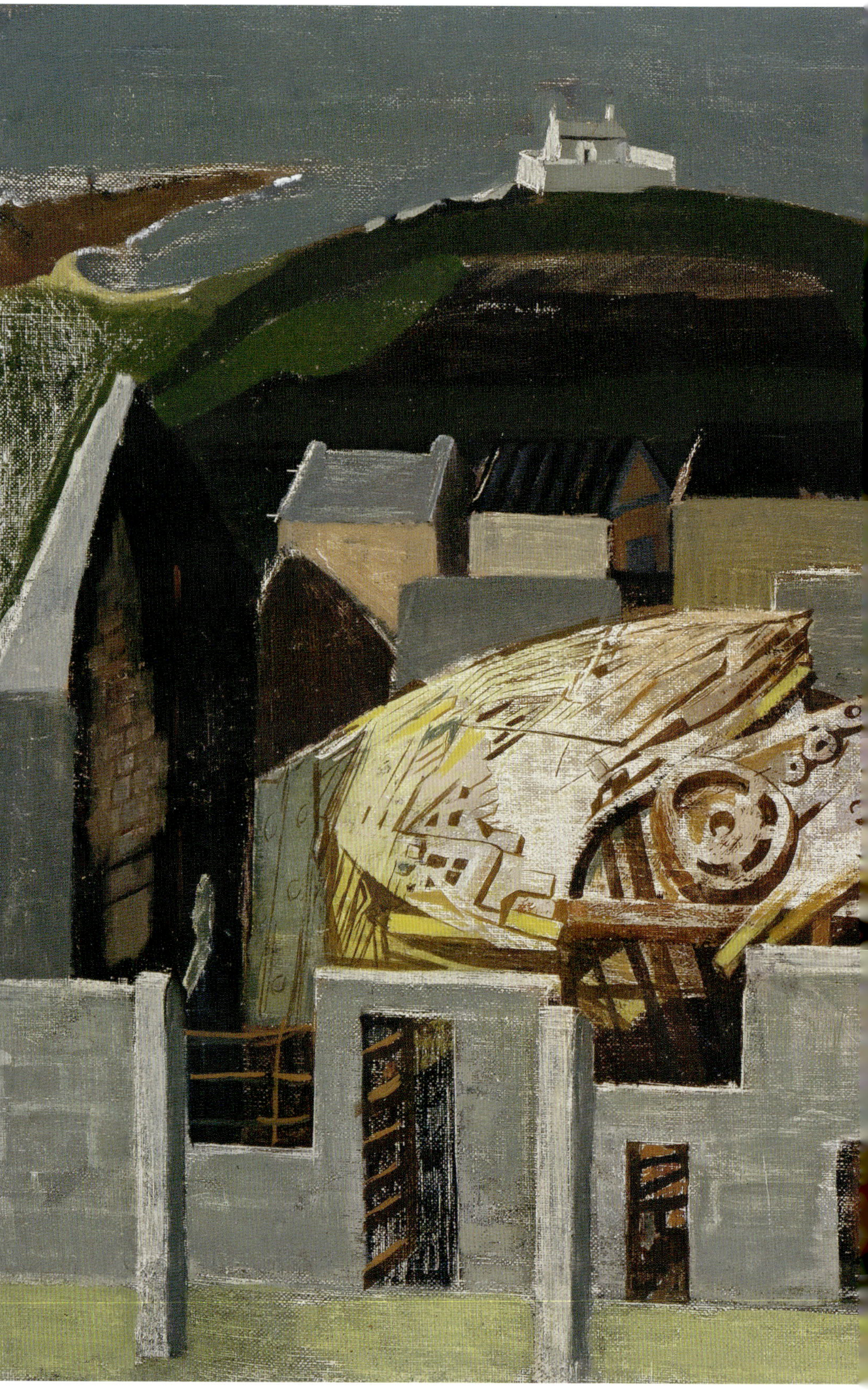

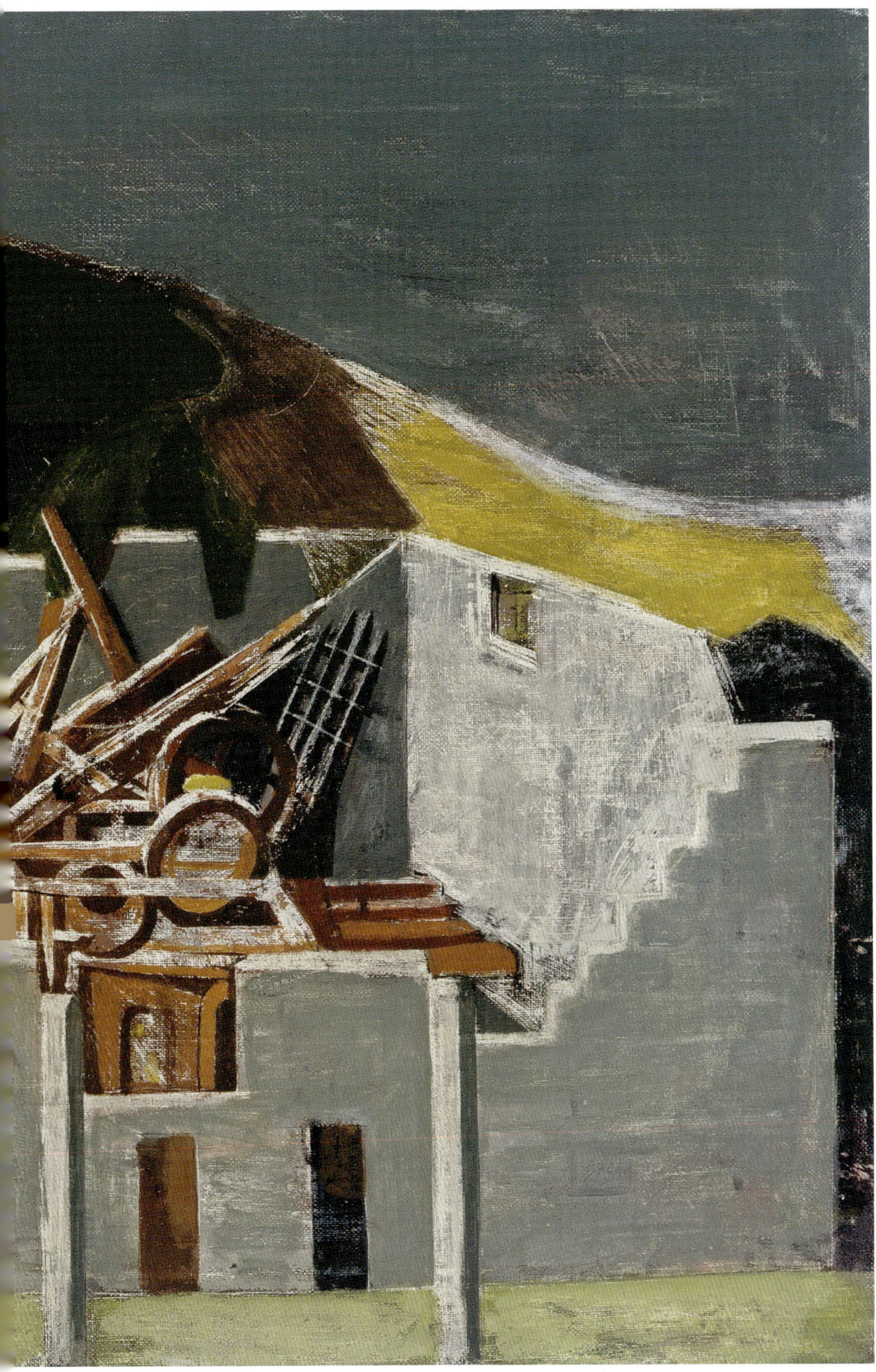

shell, protected by the land-mass from the encroaching sea. While referencing neo-romantic themes of the 1940s, it demonstrates her interest in the interior/exterior theme (at the heart of Gabo and Hepworth's work at that time) that she would fully explore in her 'Glacier' series following a trip to Switzerland in May 1949.

In the winter of 1948 she met the young poet David Lewis, recently moved to Cornwall, and despite their age difference — he was almost ten years her junior — they were married in Scotland in October 1949. Earlier that year, in February, Barns-Graham had taken part — along with younger 'Crypt Group' artists including Lanyon, Wells, Bryan Wynter (1915–1975) and Sven Berlin (1911–1999) — in the acrimonious split of the modern artists from the St Ives Society of Artists to form the new Penwith Society of Artists, led by Hepworth and Nicholson with their friend Herbert Read as its first President.[14] But the Penwith Society quickly became a forum for Lanyon's opposition to the dominance of the two senior abstract artists and the terms of membership they had devised, which split practitioners into the categories A, B and C (representational, abstract and craft). For him this was divisive, calculated to discriminate between 'traditional' and 'modern' styles of art. As a painter exploring abstraction but who continued to make representational images, Barns-Graham, nevertheless committed herself to the Penwith Society, unlike many of her peers — including Lanyon, who resigned.[15]

The rancorous, ongoing feud was unsettling for Barns-Graham. It was thanks largely to Hepworth and Nicholson's efforts and their high-level network that the south-western tip of England had become connected to the national and international art world, and as a generous friend Nicholson did his best to introduce Barns-Graham to his contacts. But Lanyon was best man at her wedding and she was attached to both sides.

Barns-Graham later came to believe that her close friendship with Nicholson, with whom she had a genuine rapport, had cost her dearly in terms of how she was perceived by her peers. From the late 1940s onwards, as the younger 'St Ives' artists became disenchanted with Nicholson and Hepworth, she was increasingly and probably deliberately excluded from group activities such as exhibition proposals and meetings with visiting dealers.[16] Worse still, she would be categorised as Nicholson's disciple. Slightly older than Lanyon and Patrick Heron (1920–1999), though roughly the same age as Frost, Wynter and Roger Hilton (1911–1975), in the catalogue accompanying the Tate Gallery's exhibition 'St Ives, 1939–64: Twenty Five Years of Painting, Sculpture and Pottery' (1985) she was omitted from this group, who were identified as the key younger generation artists. By contrast, she was noted as Nicholson's protégé:

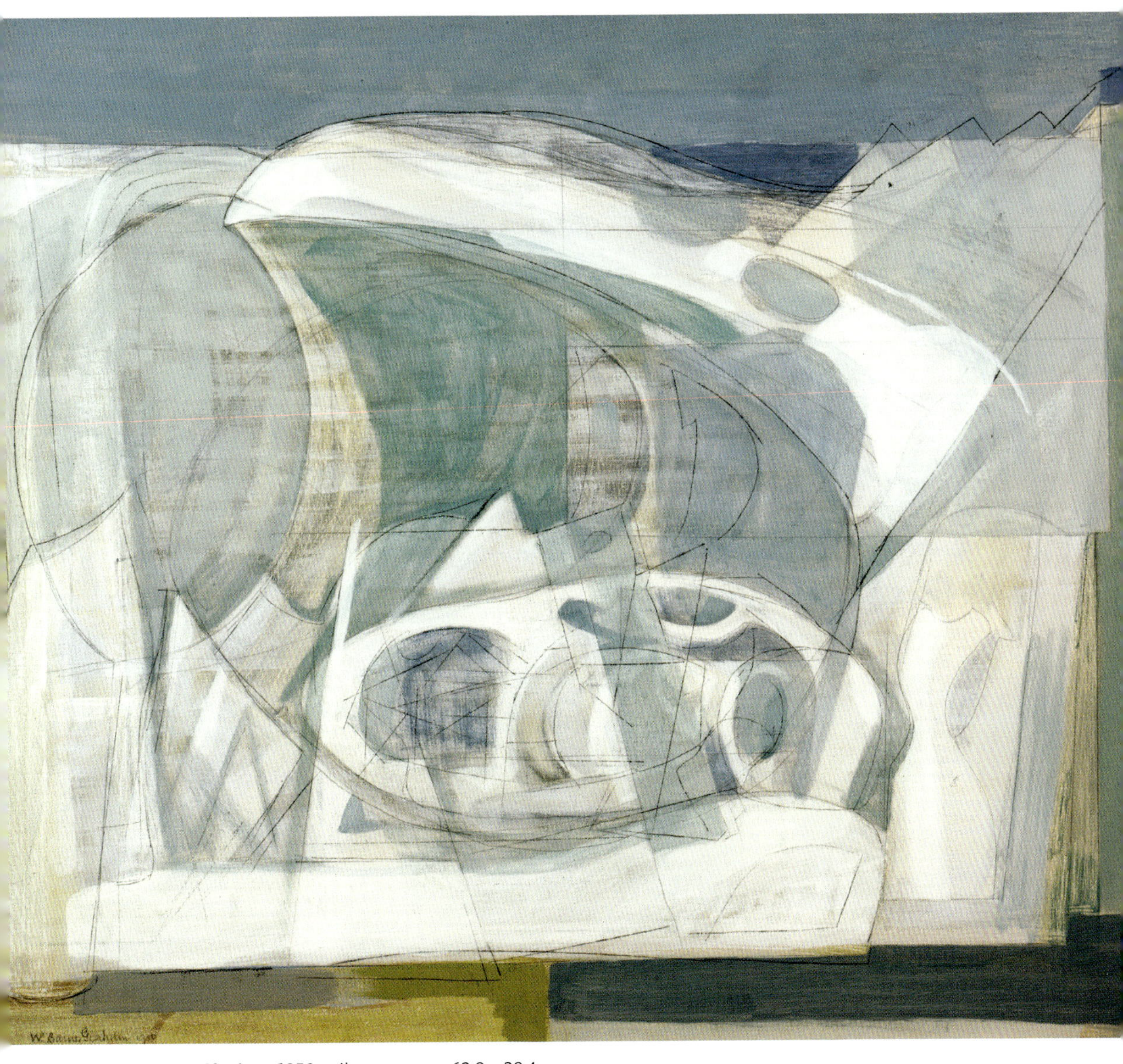

Upper Glacier · 1950 · oil on canvas · 62.9 x 39.4 cm

courtesy of the British Council Collection · photo © The British Council

Wilhelmina Barns-Graham … learnt much from Nicholson, who though never a teacher in any formal sense, had a great influence over the young artists whose work interested him.[17]

Nevertheless, for Barns-Graham — newly-wed, increasingly confident in her identity as an artist and with Europe accessible once more — the 1950s opened up exciting possibilities.

'St Ives' 1950s: towards abstraction

For the artist, this was a decade of heightened creativity, expanding horizons and critical success, as she evolved a distinctive, pared-down abstract language. Rather than blindly adopting abstraction, Barns-Graham can be seen moving across figuration and non-figuration in her work, progressing an idea in different styles simultaneously to establish her own distinctive abstraction, informed by nature's shapes, structures and underlying principles of growth.

Her experience of the Grindelwald Glacier in 1949 transformed her understanding of nature as a living force in constant flux. Through a subsequent body of work she developed a post-cubist idiom to describe space and explored the potential of abstract art to reveal the hidden dynamics of nature. Importantly, the 'Glacier' series (1949–1951; eg. p. 27) enabled her to make Gabo's and Hepworth's discoveries her own, and shows her absorbing theories of natural geometry that were gaining currency in art circles at that time, primarily the model of organic growth outlined in D'Arcy Wentworth Thompson's widely read *On Growth and Form* (1917, reprinted 1942), which acquired cult status as a source for abstract artists in the post-war period. Thompson's scientific theories beautifully illustrated the underlying relationship between the pattern, structure and growth of shells, leaves, seed heads and other natural forms and mathematical formulae such as the Golden Section (or Golden Mean). The 'Glacier' series marked a shift in her work towards abstraction, and the beginning of her preference for the Golden Section as a structure for image-making, as she later recalled:

During the late 1940s and 1950s, I experimented with the Golden Section, adapting an intersected grid on a board or canvas on which I placed one of my rock forms or glaciers or some other idea that suggested itself, sometimes using coloured chalk and pencil.[18]

Along with her colleagues she most certainly read Alan Collingridge's explanation (published in 1950) of the Golden Section as a generative ratio, for example, a Golden Section rectangle with a square removed produces another Golden

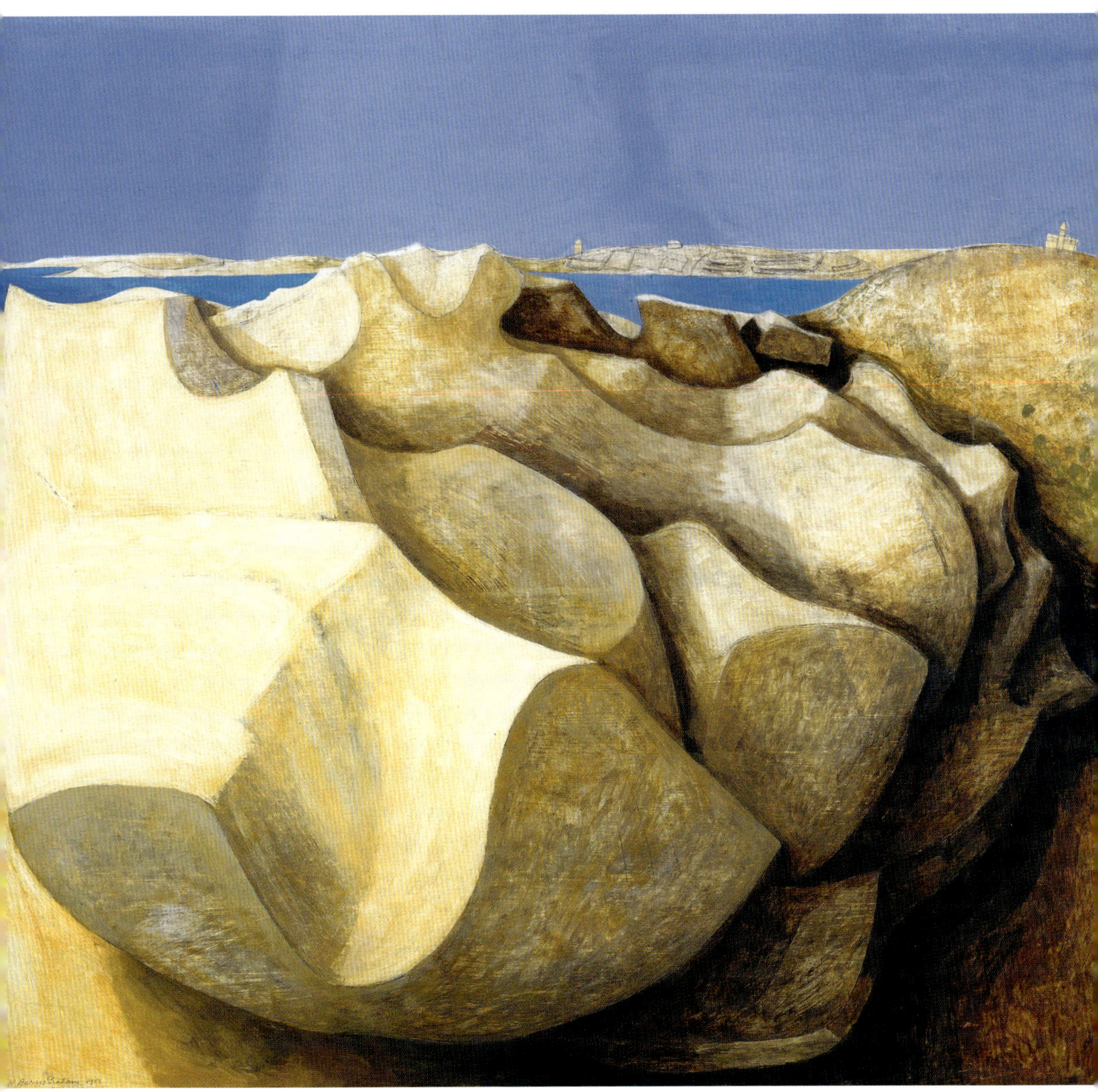

Rocks, St Mary's, Scilly Isles · 1953 · oil on board · 102.8 x 114.3 cm

City Art Centre, City of Edinburgh Museums and Galleries

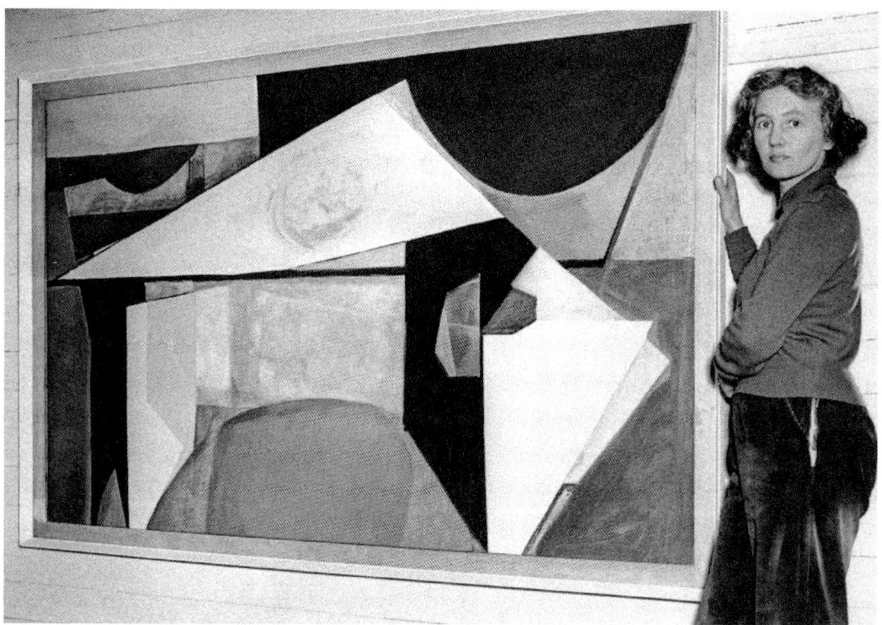

Barns-Graham with *Composition, February*, 1954

Section rectangle.[19] Natural geometry provided a means of combining her unique perception of the world with apparently objective principles or truths.

In the early 1950s, building on the momentum of the 'Glacier' theme Barns-Graham produced a series based on rock formations. Her 'Rock Forms' allude to Cornwall's mysterious, prehistoric stones and resonate with Paul Nash's images of standing stones (he died in 1949) and Hepworth's curved upright sculptures. Gradually, these evolved into grids of interlocking, outlined shapes in bold, black and white compositions such as *Rock Form* (above). As she journeyed further into abstraction she continued to draw in front of nature, to understand and feel its underlying structures, textures, colours and forms. Sometimes this led to more representational images such as *Rocks, St Mary's, Scilly Isles* (p. 29). But crucially, absorption in nature through drawing allowed her to respond intuitively and spontaneously, to discover forms that would then unconsciously emerge in her abstract paintings, as she later explained:

> *I like the loneliness of going into solitary places and studying. You find that in drawing you collect new shapes at the back of your mind, which might come out later in some form or another.*[20]

The interrelationship between her figurative and non-figurative work — the flow between representational and abstract forms — is discernible in her extensive 'Geoff and Scruffy' series (top right) also begun in the early 1950s.

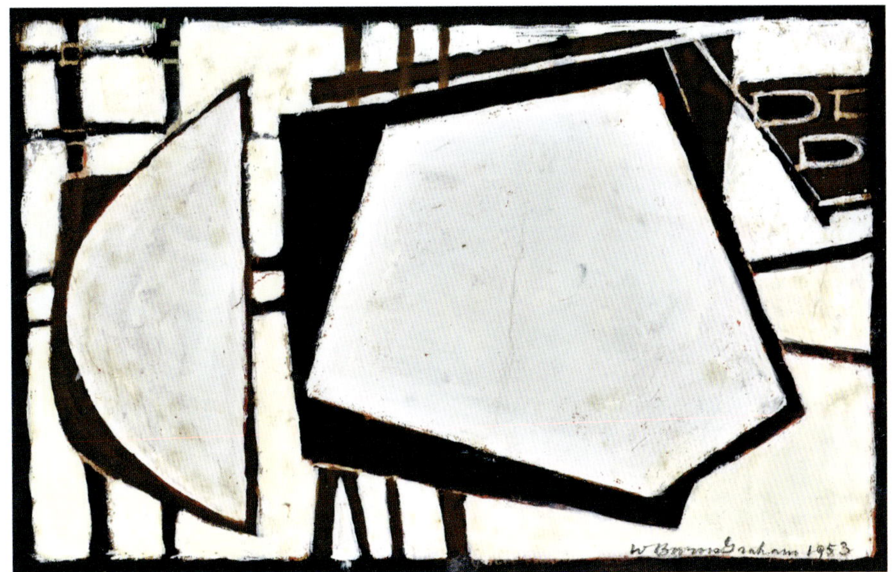

Geoff and Scruffy Series (White Images on Black, Brown and White) BGT216
1953 · mixed media on paper · 14.4 x 22.1 cm

Named after her friend Geoffrey Tribe and his dog, the series tested proportional systems, notably the Golden Section, and is characterised by the pairing of two shapes — semi-circular and pentagon — in various arrangements linked by two thin bands. The evolution of this combination of shapes can be traced in the more figurative image *Red Table* (below), with its five-sided red shape and legs.

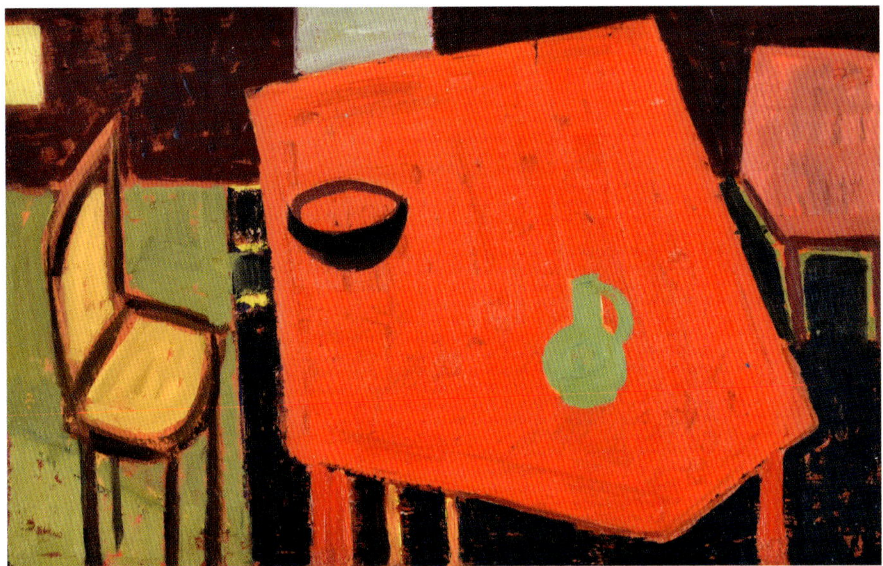

Red Table · 1952 · gouache on hardboard · 12.3 x 20 cm BGT888

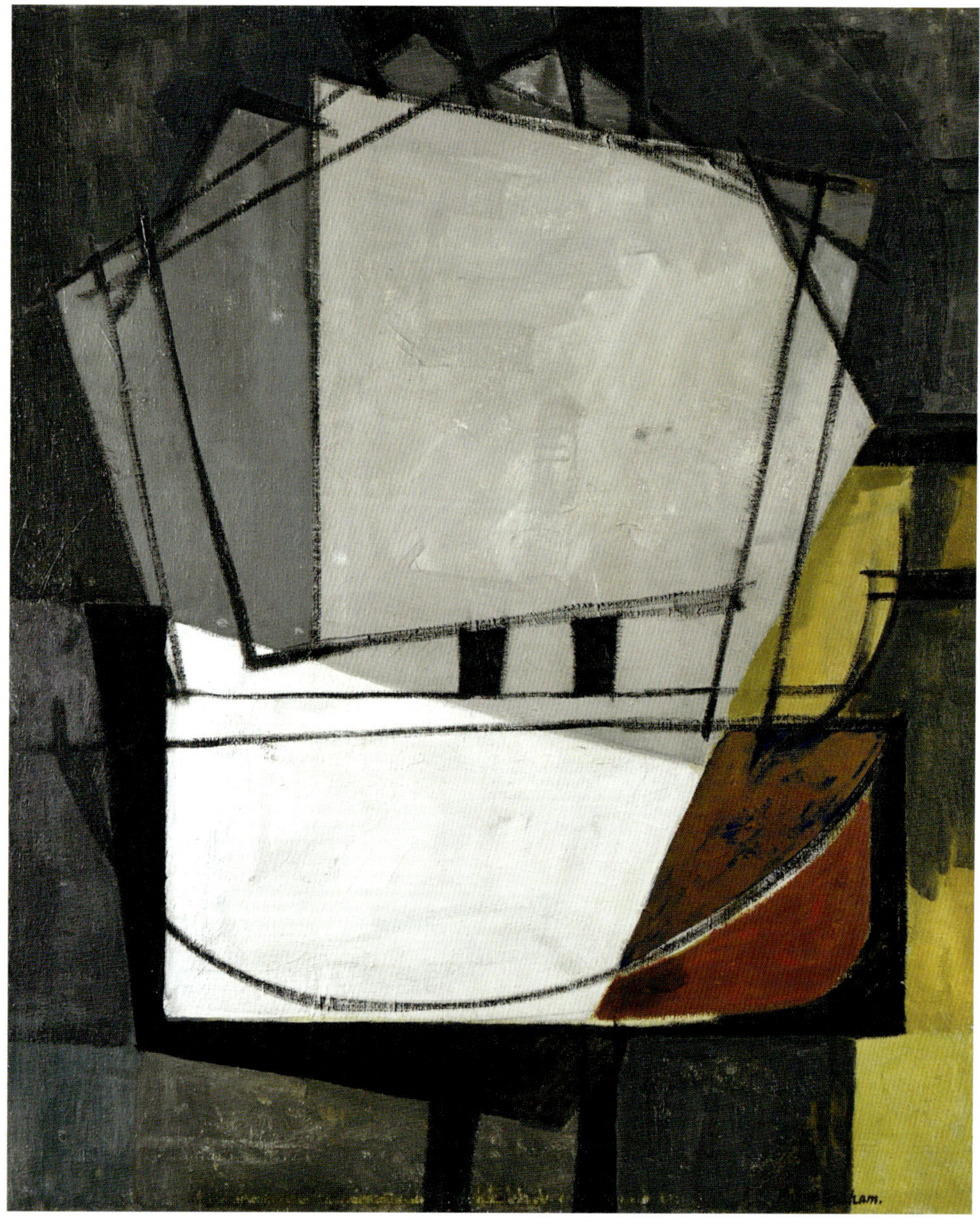

Geoff and Scruffy · 1956 · oil on canvas · 75.8 x 63.2 cm   BGT568

Experience of different places became an important part of her practice. Travelling on several occasions with her husband to Paris, the Scilly Isles and Italy gave fresh impetus to her work. In 1953 she met such artists as Alberto Giacometti (1901–1966) and Jean Arp (1886–1966) in Paris and then visited the Scilly Isles in November. The couple travelled to Italy in 1954 to attend Nicholson's exhibition at the Venice Biennale, staying in Tuscany and Siena. A series of works made in response to clay workings in Chiusure, Tuscany reveal the correspondence between Barns-Graham's studies made from observation and her developing abstract language: the shapes of the excavated earth echo the curved shapes of rock forms, and recur in the semi-circular motif in her Spanish-inspired works of the later 1950s. She returned to Italy in January 1955 on a six-month international scholarship from the Italian government, accompanied by Lewis. On the way to Milan, Rome, Sicily, Tuscany, Umbria and Campania, they stopped in Paris to visit the sculptor, Constantin Brancusi (1856–1957). Her delight in Italy's topography and architecture was captured in numerous drawings (overleaf).

Professionally, Barns-Graham was attracting attention. Her work was included in public and commercial gallery exhibitions and she was showing regularly in London, participating in such exhibitions as the ICA's 'Aspects of British Art' in December 1950, and in May the following year the Artists International Association's 'Abstract Paintings, Sculptures, Mobiles'. In January 1952 the Redfern Gallery hosted her first one-person show in London.[21] She was also exhibiting in St Ives and Scotland, with work selected for the Arts Council of Great Britain's touring show 'Seven Scottish Artists', which opened in Edinburgh in 1955. This was followed in July 1956 by her first one-person exhibition in her home country at Aitken Dott & Son, Edinburgh, with one reviewer of the show according her the accolade of 'Britain's foremost woman abstract painter'.[22]

Such exposure was matched by her inclusion in critical texts, notably J.P. Hodin's essay 'Cornish Renaissance', in *Penguin New Writing* in 1950, which reproduced two recent works and quoted her intention to visualise deeper realities through 'a process of laying bare'.[23] Read also reproduced her work in his 1951 paperback *Contemporary British Art*, aimed at the UK's growing audience for art. Her position within modern abstract art seemed further assured by reference to her work in Michel Seuphor's *A Dictionary of Abstract Painting* (1956, English translation 1957) and the revised edition in 1957 of R.H. Wilenski's classic text on modernism, *The Modern Movement in Art* (1927). Wilenski aligned her with such artists as Frost, Gear, Victor Pasmore (1908–1998) and Pierre Soulages (b.1919), for their shared concern with combining universal geometric beauty and subjective organic rhythm.[24] But while her professional life took off, privately her marriage was unravelling.

In autumn 1956 Lewis enrolled to study architecture full-time in Leeds. She followed him there, invited by Harry Thubron (1915–1985) at Leeds School of Art to teach life drawing and painting part-time. Although she only taught for one session, her work was selected for exhibitions in Leeds, Bradford and Wakefield, with *Snow at Wharfdale I* (1957) eliciting favourable critical attention.[25] The newly introduced Basic Design course at Leeds also stimulated her thinking, contributing to her adoption of a more systems-based abstraction in the 1960s and 1970s. Its progressive pedagogy emphasised experimentation, encouraging students to develop creativity through making, guided by a sequence of exercises that investigated the principal elements of visual art and their inherent dynamics. The Golden Section — already familiar to Barns-Graham — was taught as a core element and she used it with new confidence in such paintings as *White, Black and Yellow (Composition February)* (right) to structure highly-charged arrangements of diagonal poles.[26] Yet, like the abstract paintings of Piet Mondrian (1872–1944), this work also suggests a frozen, northern landscape with a cold, grey horizon.

Despite these promising professional developments, in Leeds the crisis in her marriage escalated. She returned to St Ives in 1957 for what she thought would be a six-month trial separation, but the couple remained apart. The marriage

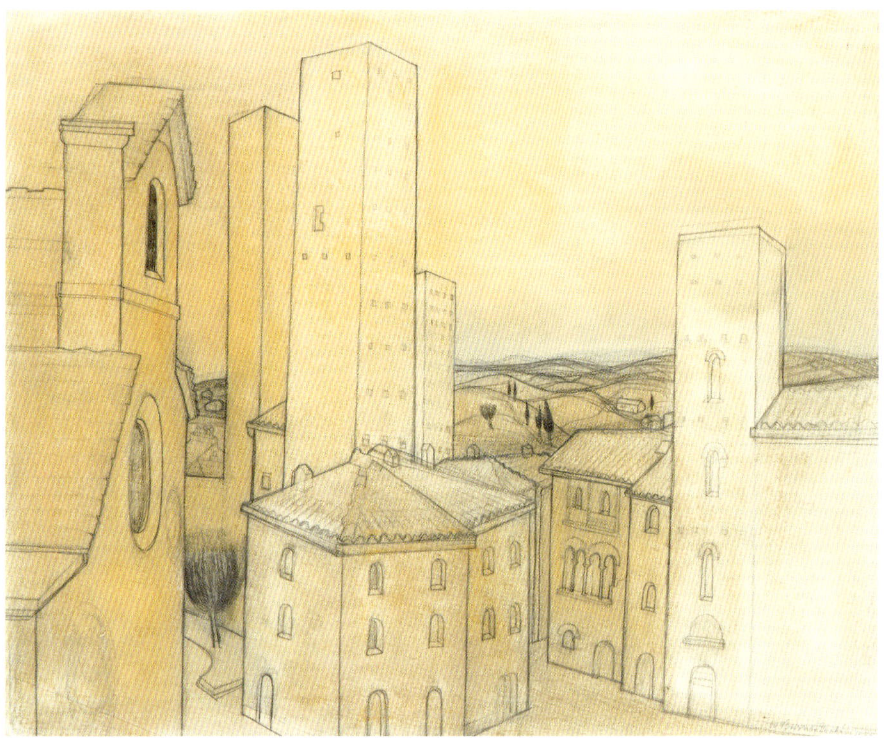

San Gimignano · 1955 · pencil and oil on paper · 42.6 x 54.9 cm   BGT2302

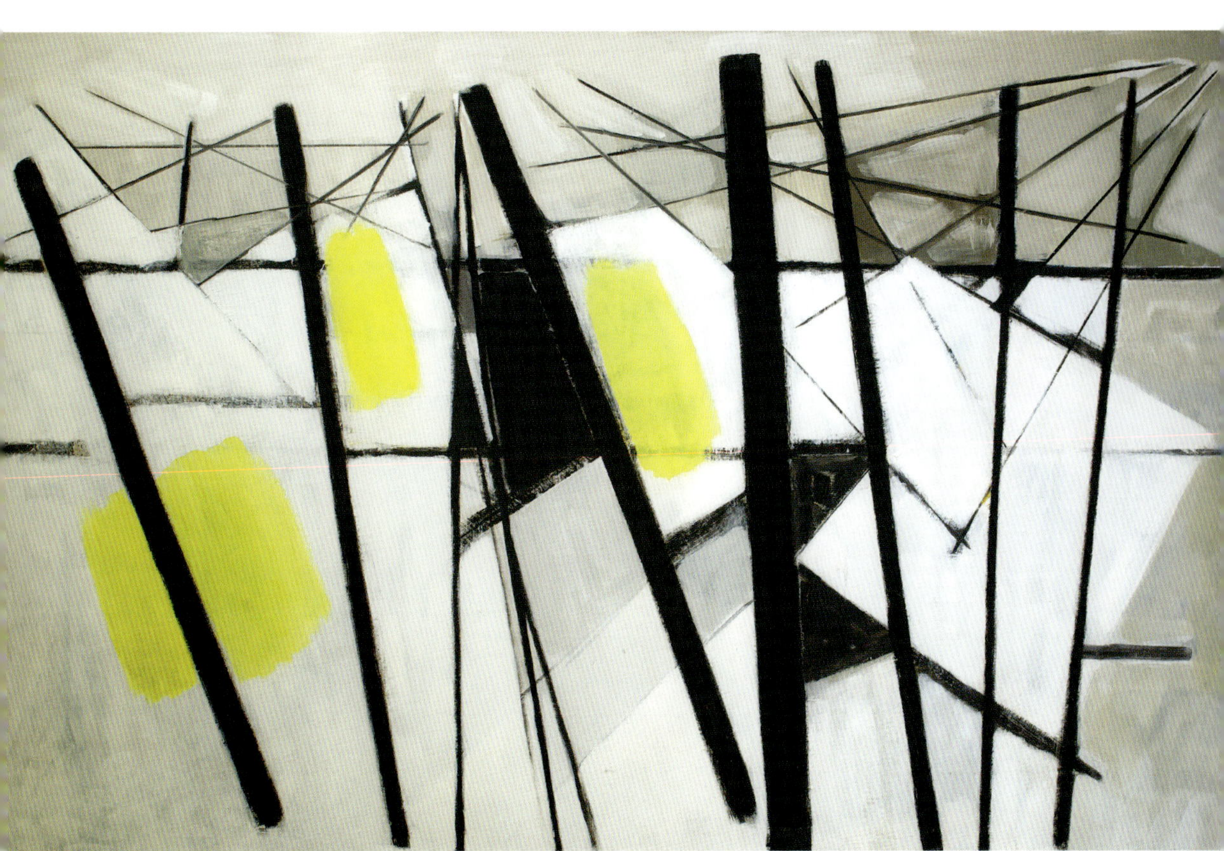

White, Black and Yellow (Composition February) · 1957 · oil on canvas · 122 x 198 cm
Tate · presented by Wilhelmina Barns-Graham Trust with Art Fund support 2018 · T15052

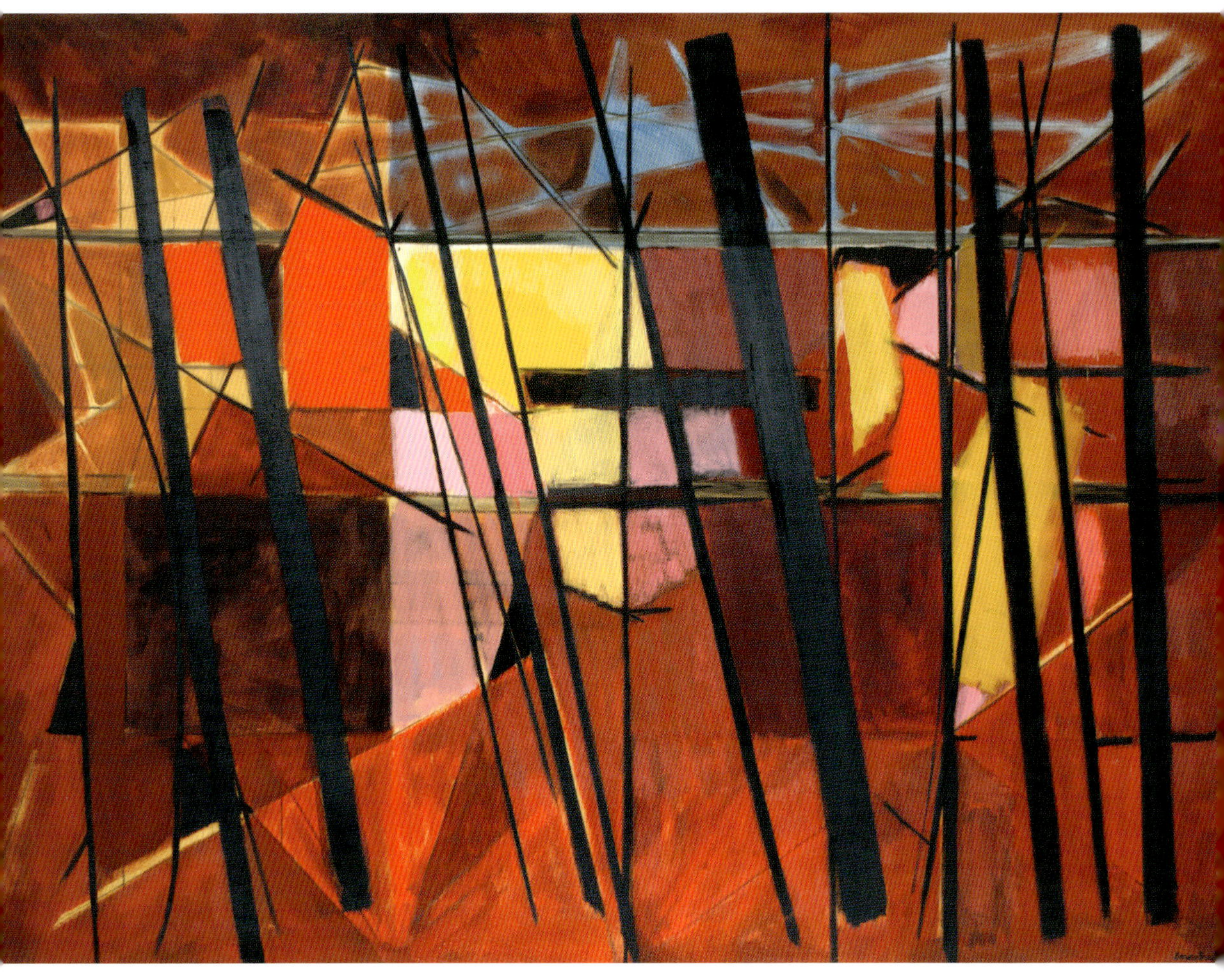

Red Painting · 1957 · oil on canvas · 102 x 152.5 cm

was annulled in 1963, and after completing his studies Lewis left for the United States with someone else's wife.

Red Painting (left) was also made for the exhibition in Wakefield. While its rhythmic poles reflect her growing interest in the mathematical relationships between dynamic forms — a concern that would dominate her work in the 1960s — the painting's agitated lines and strident colour have frequently been interpreted as an expression of her emotional state at that time.

According to Green, the break-up of the marriage was 'a devastating blow' that coloured her emotional and artistic life for years after. She was plagued by a sense of failure, and possibly shame, as divorce was then unthinkable for the Barns-Graham family.[27] Her father died in 1957, and the following year Nicholson left St Ives for Switzerland with his third wife Felicitas Vogler, never to return. The mounting sense of loss was overwhelming.

'St Ives': a woman's place

It is unlikely that any woman artist would have been fully accepted as part of the post-war 'St Ives' gang of younger male artists. The camaraderie between the key protagonists is evidenced by the well-known Christmas card collage from Lanyon to Frost, depicting them both with Wynter, Hilton and Heron against the harbour in St Ives. The 1950s were characterised by a renascent male chauvinism that affected social life and social relations. Pubs, for example, were key meeting places for artists in St Ives, but they were unwelcoming places for unaccompanied women.[28] In a period of ongoing rationing and austerity times were hard, especially for aspiring artists with large families to feed. Anecdotal evidence suggests that women artists selling their work were resented by male artists as this undermined their own capacity for sales.[29]

Even though Lewis and Barns-Graham also scraped a living in the 1950s, she was a childless, married woman from a relatively privileged upper-class background, who had benefited from an extended art education. By contrast a number of the younger male artists were from working class backgrounds or had served in the war, coming to art later through the ex-serviceman's grant. Her commercial success flouted gender stereotypes at that time.

Barns-Graham's marriage had further aligned her with Nicholson and Hepworth. Lewis became Hepworth's secretary and the Penwith Society's curator (1951–54), also acting as a quasi-agent in St Ives for the British Council and the Arts Council, which Barns-Graham felt caused resentment locally, as did his position as a critic and writer.[30] For example, when in April 1951 Lewis favourably reviewed the 'Glacier' paintings in the *St Ives Times*, poet Arthur Caddock commented that this was another way of saying 'His family's doing nicely.' As Michael Bird has observed, such comments reveal the double standard at work in St Ives, where women (including Barns-Graham) were often supporting their artist husbands, while a man promoting his wife's paintings was ridiculed.[31]

The increasing scale of paintings in the 1950s, encouraged by the example of American Abstract Expressionism, has also been associated with an assertive, post-war masculinity. Barns-Graham became interested in the work of such American painters as Robert Motherwell (1915–1991) and Adolph Gottlieb (1903–1974) and produced some larger works from the 1950s onwards. But preferring to work with dimensions commensurate with her diminutive 5' 2" frame, she may well have felt disadvantaged by the scale required of serious art during the 1950s and 1960s. Nedira Yakir has reported that Barns-Graham intentionally made larger paintings — especially at the end of her life — to challenge assumptions about women's art, as acts of defiance against gender and age.[32]

During the 1940s and 1950s many of the 'St Ives' artists were sharing similar sources and themes, including the Cornish landscape and environment. Under Roger Hilton's influence the focus on landscape shifted; for example, Frost began increasingly to explore the theme of the sexualised female body, while Lanyon before his untimely death in 1964 was responding to the new direction of Pop Art. Like her friend Hilton, Barns-Graham was committed to art as a means of giving form to sensations and feelings, whether this was through abstraction or figuration. But possibly to assert herself as an artist in a male-dominated arena and to resist the 'derogatory feminine', as articulated by Hepworth, she may have unconsciously gravitated towards masculine subjects and themes — muscular rocks, powerful forces, science — and abstraction, which signified a degree of philosophical and intellectual rigour.[33] Her mid-career work certainly suggests an internal tussle between what might have been regarded as masculine rationality and intuitive, feminine impulses.

1960s and 1970s: meditations and experiments

In her middle decades Barns-Graham's relationship to the two main strands of so-called process-dominant art — Constructionism and Tachisme or Action Painting — remained ambivalent. Process-dominant or systems-based art describes an approach in which the artwork is determined through the protocols of its making, rather than by any other intention imposed by the artist. Emerging in the late 1940s, it was governed either by depersonalised geometric systems (Constructionist) or by mark-making through which the

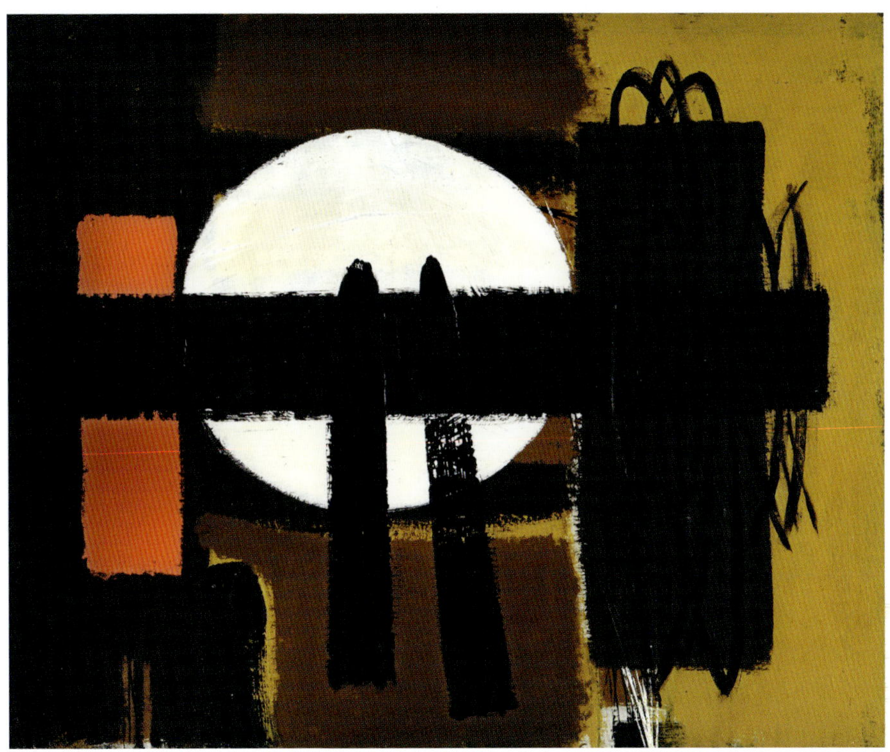

Spanish Coast No. 3 (Spanish Island Series)
1958–9 · oil on canvas · 67 x 84.5 cm

BGT6406

artist interacts with materials (Tachisme/Action Painting).[34] From the mid-1960s until the late 1970s, Barns-Graham's work was dominated by a systems-based approach to abstraction, perhaps guided by an unconscious decision to shield herself from overpowering, negative emotions. But throughout this period she continued to draw from nature and to work intuitively, following her need for 'psychic release'.[35]

As a coping mechanism during her separation from Lewis, for three years Barns-Graham removed herself from St Ives, renting a studio in London. In 1963 she returned to St Ives, purchasing a combined studio residence, No. 1 Barnaloft, in a recently converted fish loft facing Porthmeor beach, which remained her home. In 1960 she also inherited Balmungo, her Aunt Mary's house and estate near St Andrews, and subsequently lived there for three months each winter. However, travelling between the two places further isolated Barns-Graham from 'St Ives', compounding her sense of being a 'lone wolf'. She was particularly introspective during the early 1960s, turning to psychoanalytic theory, philosophy and religion. For a decade she joined the annual Cornish pilgrimage to the Shrine of Our Lady of Walsingham in Norfolk and in 1965 she became a member of the Anglican Church. Although her attachment to formal religion didn't last, she

Black Oval · 1957–9 · oil on canvas · 84.2 x 102.8 cm   BGT6465

held on to a reflective spiritual awareness. All of this helped her overcome the anguish and disorientation of divorce.[36]

Her work in the early 1960s was influenced by a visit to Spain and the Balearic Islands in 1958. She made lively drawings of Formentera's contorted rocky coastline, and – combined with the example of Miró's paintings in Barcelona – this had a loosening effect on her work. She adopted a sinuous brushstroke and a palette inspired by the earthy colours associated with Spain (eg. *Spanish Coast No. 3*, p. 39). Away from St Ives, Barns-Graham also experimented with the gestural potential of American Abstract Expressionism, which was exerting its influence in Britain through transatlantic friendships, exhibitions and critical discourse. She was attracted to the use of the brushstroke as an abstract motif – its reference to traditional Japanese and Chinese painting techniques invoking a spiritual meaning or inflection – and produced some radically simplified compositions that prefigure later work, notably *Black Oval* (above).[37]

The move to Barnaloft dovetailed with the beginnings of a radical departure in her work that would last for at least a decade, namely the series 'Order and Disorder of Things of a Kind'. Ostensibly an investigation of the expressive properties of shapes and colours through their interaction in different

combinations, for Barns-Graham the interdependency of these formal elements
provided metaphors for relationships in the world, between things and people.
Using mathematical frameworks to establish ordered arrangements of abstract
motifs — typically the square or circle — she then offset them to create a sense
of movement. Irregular rhythms triggered chain reactions of disorder and
suggested cause and effect (eg. *Progression*, overleaf). Through preparatory
studies she experimented, adjusting colour choices until the overall image
looked and felt right (eg. *Ascending Squares of Equal Amount*, p. 43).

Barns-Graham's increasing reliance on proportional systems and her admir-
ation for Klee's work and writings during these decades links her to the group
of London-based constructionist artists that emerged around Victor Pasmore
in the 1950s.[38] Since the late 1940s, Pasmore had advocated abstraction as a
method of construction determined by proportional systems, rather than a
process of abstracting forms from nature.[39] Although she knew Pasmore, Barns-
Graham's closest connection with the group was through her friend, the sculptor
Robert Adams (1917–1984). But while she shared the constructionist interest in
the correspondence of mathematical formula to the physical world, she never
abandoned human perception and feeling in her work, and continued to use
the Golden Section as an underlying framework on which she could elaborate.[40]
A later comment reveals the relationship between her constructed abstractions
and her perception of natural phenomena:

> *At the end of the 50s, partly due to the events in my life and my philosophical
> and theological ideas at this period, I became involved with formal relationships.
> 'Order and Disorder of Things of a Kind' was such a theme. I used the progression
> of a single square to several circles, egg-forms, oblongs, lines following each other
> in pen and ink, breaking the rhythm deliberately or by accident, simple wave
> movements, cell formations, bird flights, fish shoals, backs of fern leaves, dots
> inside foxgloves, rain drops, leaves in the wind, diamonds on water, human
> gatherings.[41]*

Barns-Graham's repetition of units such as the square, combined with
a strong palette of primaries and their complementary colours, generates a
visual vibration that invites comparison with Op Art of the 1960s. However her
interest lay in the failure of a structure, rather than in a systematic repetition.[42]
Other works from the 'Things of a Kind' series, such as *Dance of the Thermals*
(1964) and *Assembly of Nine* (1964), are even less schematic, reflecting her
interest in celestial and spiritual themes.

In the 1970s she continued to focus on geometric shapes but with a greater
emphasis on colour, light and mood. For example, *Lime Green, Orange and*

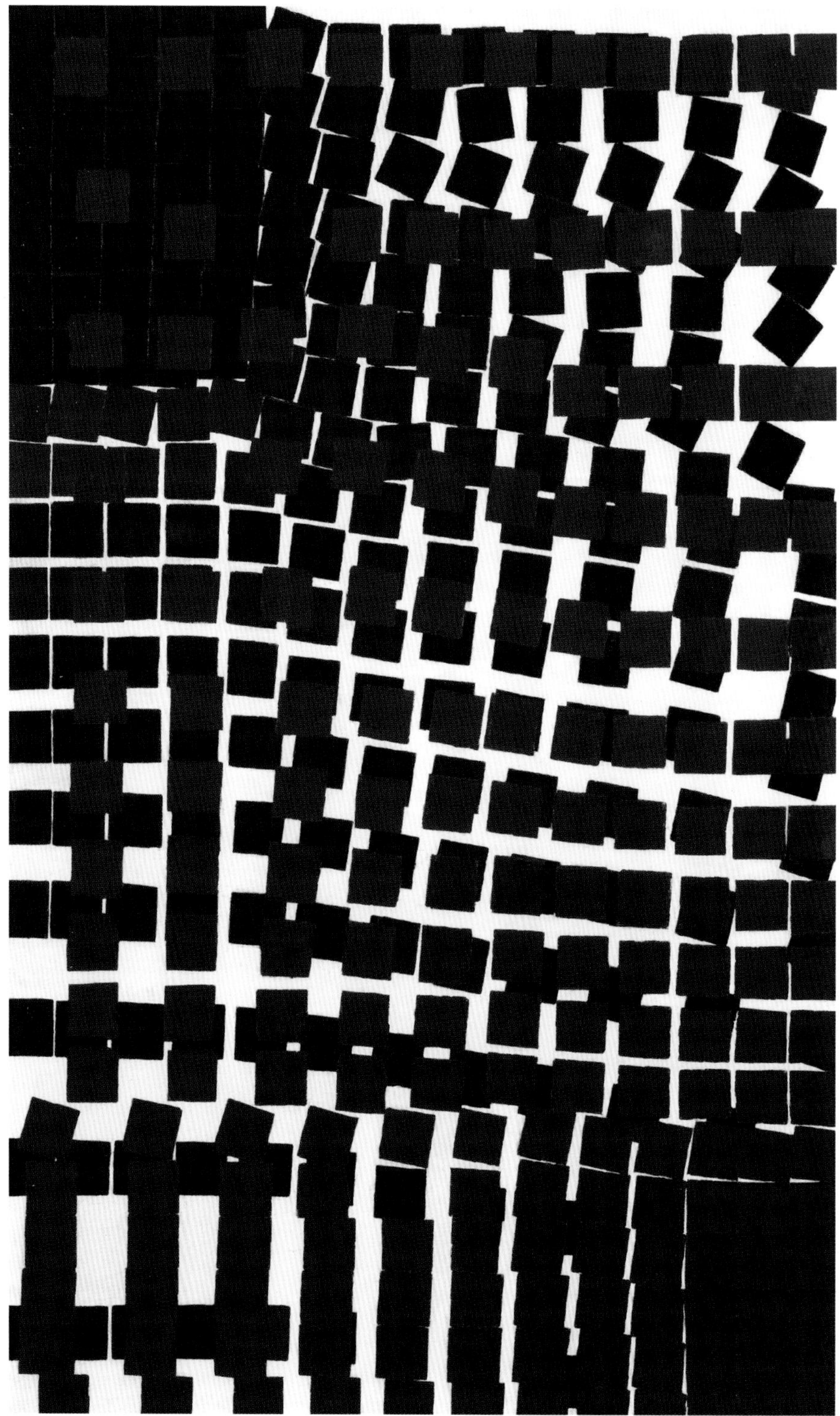

Progression · 1965 · oil on board · 197.5 x 121.5 cm

Leeds Museums and Galleries (Leeds Art Gallery) · presented by Wilhelmina Barns-Graham Trust with Art Fund support 2019

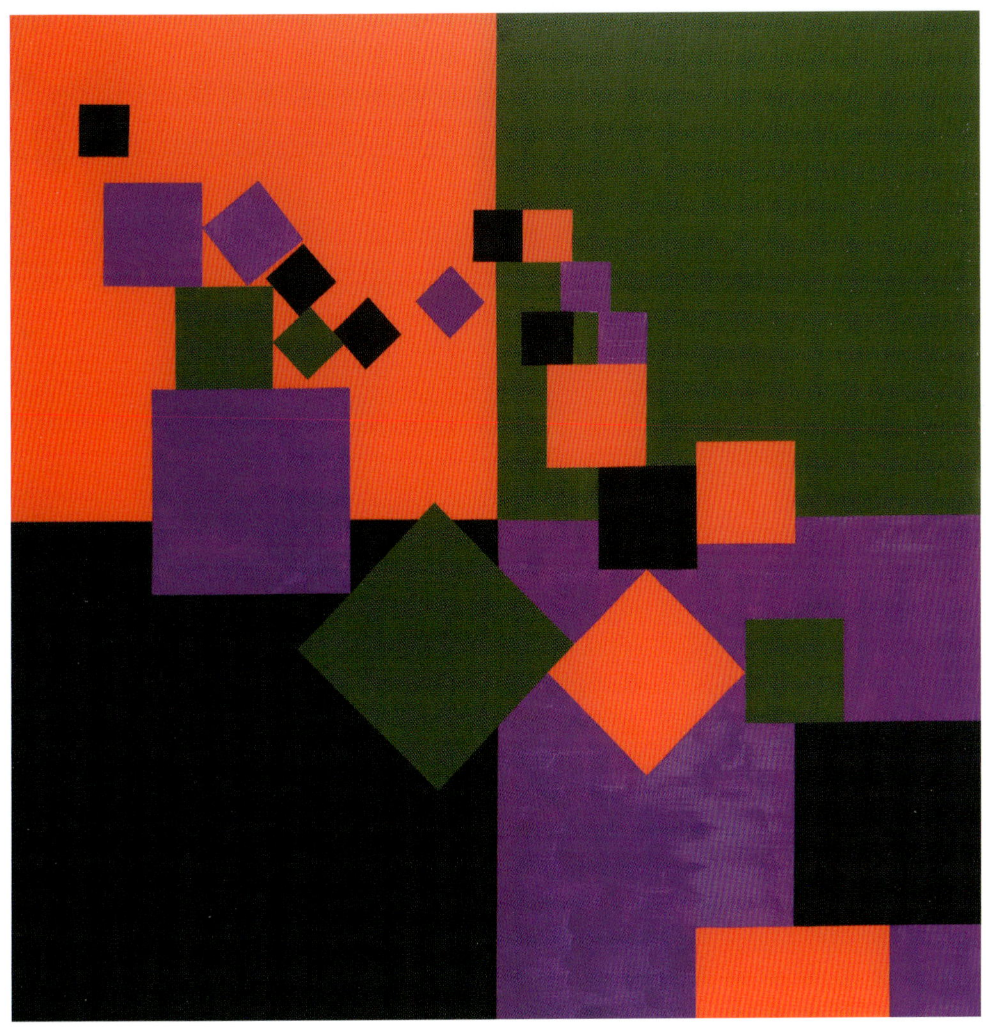

Ascending Squares of Equal Amount · 1970 · oil on canvas · 122 x 121 cm

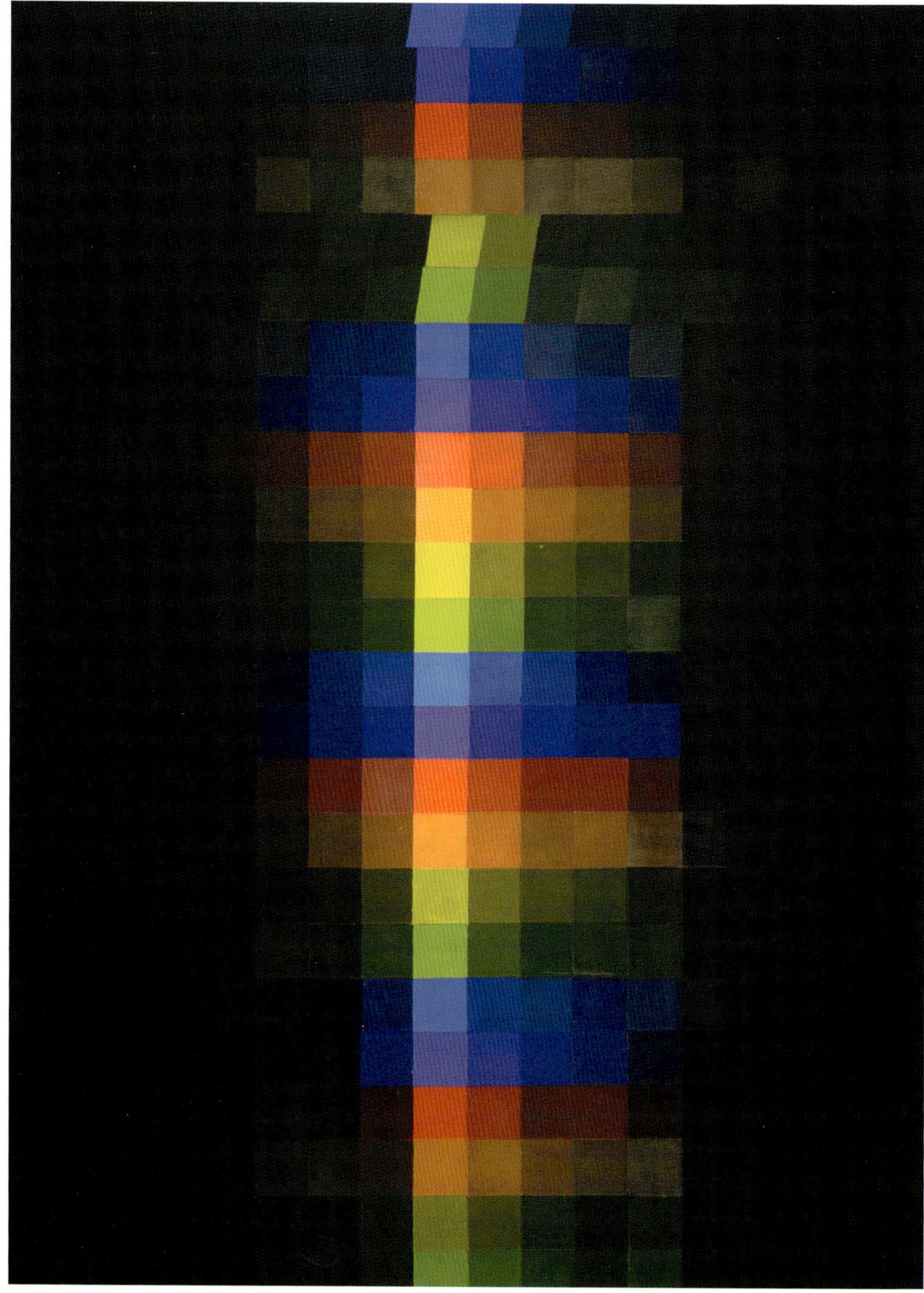

More or Less (Meditation 4) · 1978 · acrylic on canvas · 122.4 x 92 cm   BGT384

Blue Mediterranean (below) highlights colour sensation, which she explored further in her 'Meditation' series of the late 1970s (left). From 1973 the artist Rowan James (1937–2005) became her studio assistant and an important fixture in Barns-Graham's life, managing the Balmungo estate, overseeing her business affairs and providing emotional support. In 1989 Barns-Graham wrote of her 'sense of increasing freedom and strength' in her work.[43] This renewed optimism was facilitated by James, who alleviated the burden of managing her professional and domestic life alone in old age.

Alongside her essays in pure colour, Barns-Graham's life-long fascination with the forms and forces of nature persisted, largely through drawings of the hypnotic movement of the sea that she observed in St Ives and St Andrews. The motion of waves and the impact of wind on water can also be seen in the ambitious 'Expanding Forms' series of the early 1980s (eg. overleaf), worked out on a mathematical basis. But her acute observation of the ocean over many years

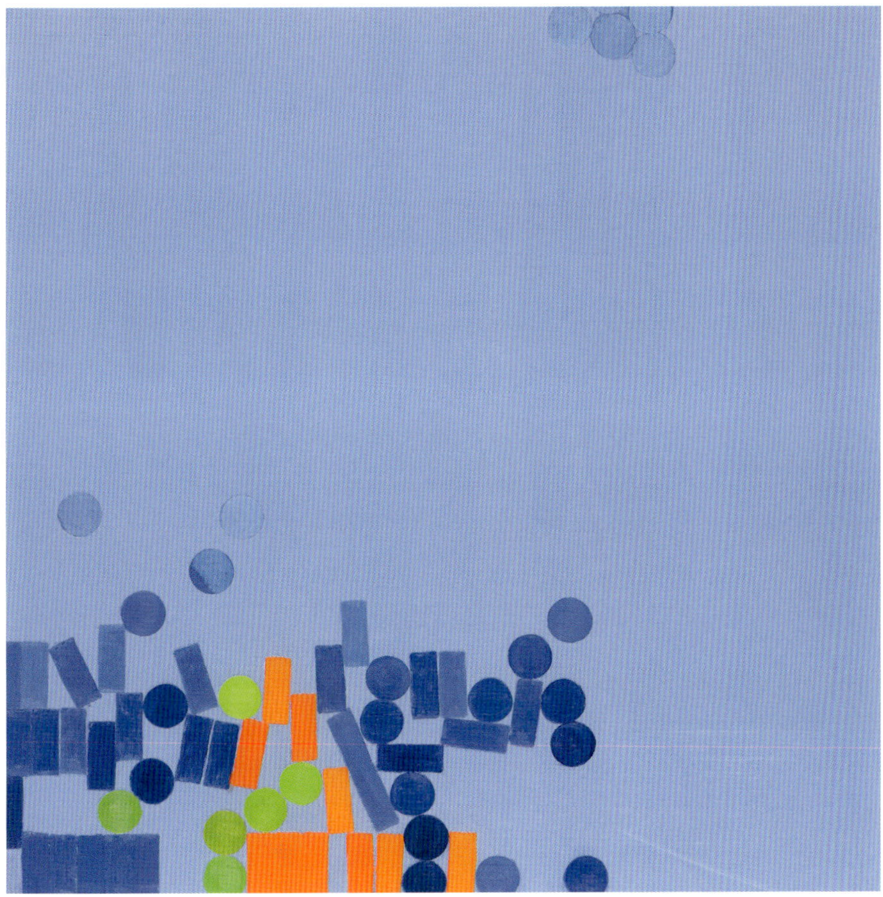

Lime Green, Orange and Blue Mediterranean
1972 · oil on hardboard · 50.6 x 50.7 cm

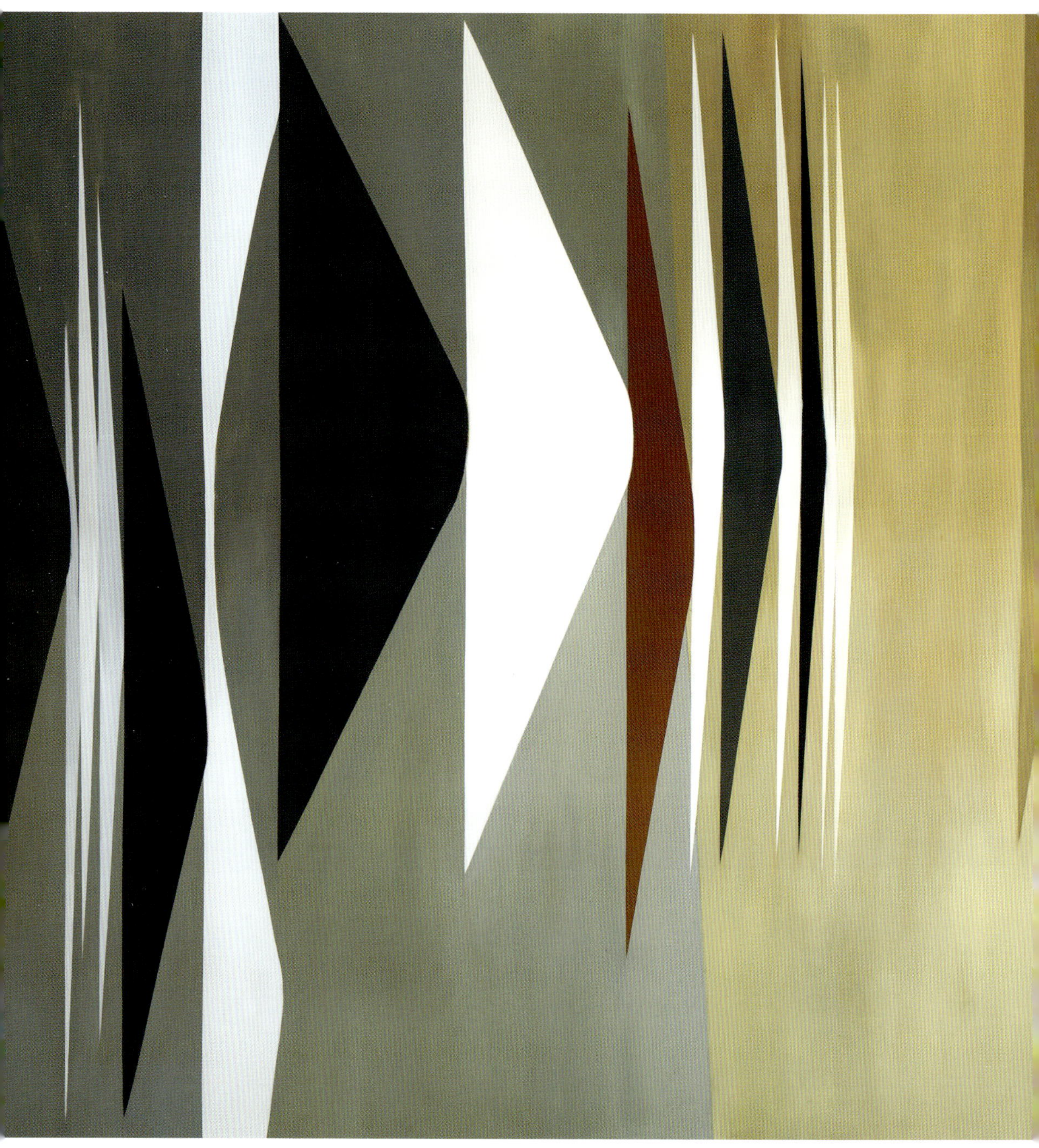

Expanding Forms (Coast) Touch Point Series No. 6 · 1981 · oil on canvas · 152 x 152 cm BGT474

found perfect expression in the iconic line drawings of the 1970s and 1980s that eloquently describe the movement of sand and waves (*Eight Lines, Porthmeor*, p. 68).[44] In paintings she also expressed the physical sensation and universal meaning of other elemental phenomena such as wind and fire.

Although she continued to exhibit — for example, in 1961 her work was selected for group shows in New York, Canada and Sweden — during these middle decades she rarely had one-person shows and felt her career had been eclipsed by those of other 'St Ives' artists.

1980s and later decades: a 'looking in-looking out'[45] kind of artist
After experiencing the pleasure of critical attention in the 1950s, Barns-Graham's sense of neglect was exacerbated by the Tate Gallery's important St Ives exhibition of 1985, which included only three of her works. But the end of the decade brought renewed interest in her work, particularly in Scotland, where she enjoyed her first retrospective in 1989 at Edinburgh's City Art Centre. In a statement published the previous year, Barns-Graham seemed to anticipate the direction that her work would take for the remainder of her life, explaining that abstraction more than any other approach allowed her to express her 'idea', or 'inner perception':

> *The positive aspect of working in an abstract way for me, is the freedom of choice, i.e. medium, space, texture, colours, the challenge of feeling out the truth of an idea — a process of inner perception and harmony of thought on a high level.*
> *Abstraction is a wide field, and it is not [all] necessarily Abstract. Both involve ideas. Abstract is a refinement and greater discipline to the idea, truth to the medium thus perfecting the idea, only using that which perfects or adds to that idea.[46]*

In the mid-1980s, having adhered primarily to systems-based painting for a number of decades she was ready for change. The retrospective was timely, rekindling her interest in the 'Geoff and Scruffy' series and Spanish paintings of the 1960s, with their calligraphic marks, circles and rich palette. It allowed her to reassess and cross-fertilise, to mine her own visual repertoire. As previously in her career, unfamiliar landscapes also provided creative stimulus, and after twenty-five years she resumed the practice of making study trips, for example to Orkney and Lanzarote, to generate new bodies of work in a range of media including drawings, paintings and reliefs. Dramatically formed by volcanic activity, Lanzarote's terrain embodied raw geomorphological process, no doubt triggering memories of the expanding and contracting glacier encountered years before in Switzerland.

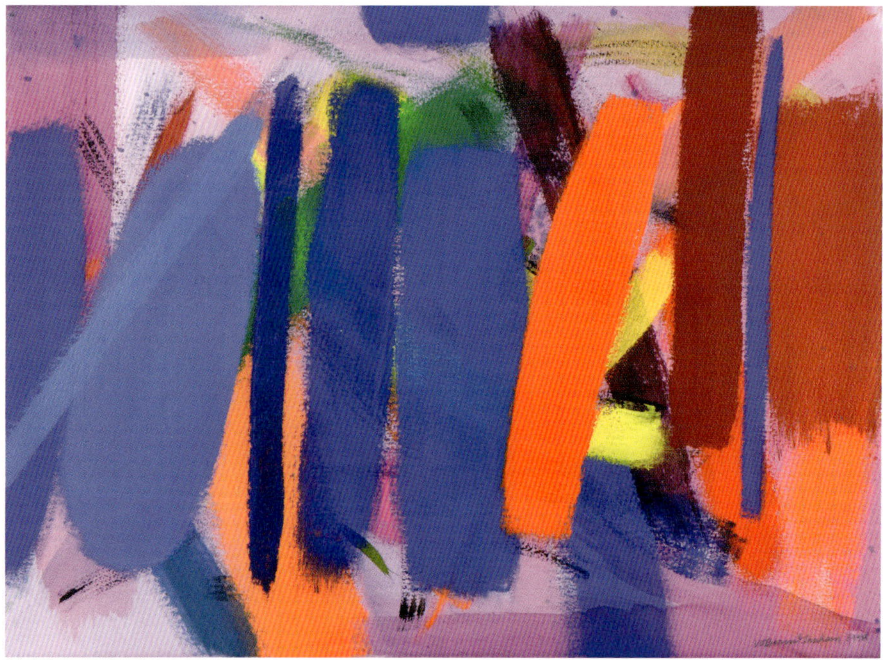

Blue Dance · 1998 · acrylic on paper · 57.5 x 76.3 cm   BGT949

Remarkably, from her eighties and until her death, Barns-Graham's desire to make work accelerated. Following a period struggling with illness in the mid-1980s and appreciating her mortality, she embarked on a series of exuberant abstract paintings and silkscreen prints, in which saturated colour and line are integrated in large, gestural brushstrokes to celebrate life and nature. Barns-Graham's practice had been governed by a certain rigour and professionalism both in her general attitude and in her daily habits as an artist. She had a strong sense of the artist's metier. While she lost none of this discipline in her later years, she relaxed the self-imposed constraints in her work. She set up harmonies and rhythms using proportional frameworks, but colour became the main protagonist as she delighted in her unique synesthetic perception of the world (eg. *Blue Dance*, above).[47]

In 1988 at the Tate Gallery's 'Late Picasso' exhibition she was moved by the energy and risk-taking displayed by the artist at the end of his life. Her mother's death in 1989 also heightened her own sense that time was running out. In these late works, which might be understood as 'direct speech' in visual form, she felt she had finally found her voice, and was determined to sing unreservedly, reminded of Psalm 100: 'Come before His presence with a song'.[48] Some of the debilitating effects of physical decline were overcome through her close collaboration with Carol Robertson and Robert Adam of the Graal Press. Their innovative silkscreen printing techniques allowed her to build an image in layers, with control over formal structure and proportion, and to amass a personal collection of reusable marks.[49]

Reflecting on her career in the 1990s, Barns-Graham consistently cast herself as a 'lone wolf', never quite fitting in, preferring to follow her own instincts and interests. On one level, applied retrospectively this persona may have helped her account for and deal with the deeply-felt sense of rejection she experienced from the 1960s onwards, when she disappeared from a central narrative of British modern art. But in some respects, 'lone wolf' accurately describes her modus operandi. She succeeded in pursuing the artist's life at a time when few women achieved this. Seeking a middle ground between systems and her senses, she used the visual language of abstraction to express something real about the perceived world. In this she may have been guided by Picasso's example. Writing in 1936, Herbert Read argued that avoiding a doctrinaire attitude towards making art had allowed Picasso to draw on nature's 'vital sources of inspiration', quoting the artist:

> *There is no abstract art. We must always begin with something ... Whether he likes it or not, man is an instrument of nature; she imposes her character and appearance on him ... We cannot contradict nature. She is stronger than the strongest of men! We can allow ourselves some liberties; but only in details.*[50]

Through developing her own abstract vocabulary of line, form and colour Barns-Graham was able to capture her total experience of nature, and transform her outer perceptions of the world through the filter of her inner feelings, memories and emotions. With growing critical and commercial success in her eighties, along with honorary doctorates from St Andrews, Plymouth, Exeter and Heriot Watt Universities, Barns-Graham's contribution to British art was further recognised with a CBE in 2001. She died in St Andrews on 26 January 2004, aged 91, having succeeded in her ambition to visualise the world as perceived and felt through her eye, hand and heart.

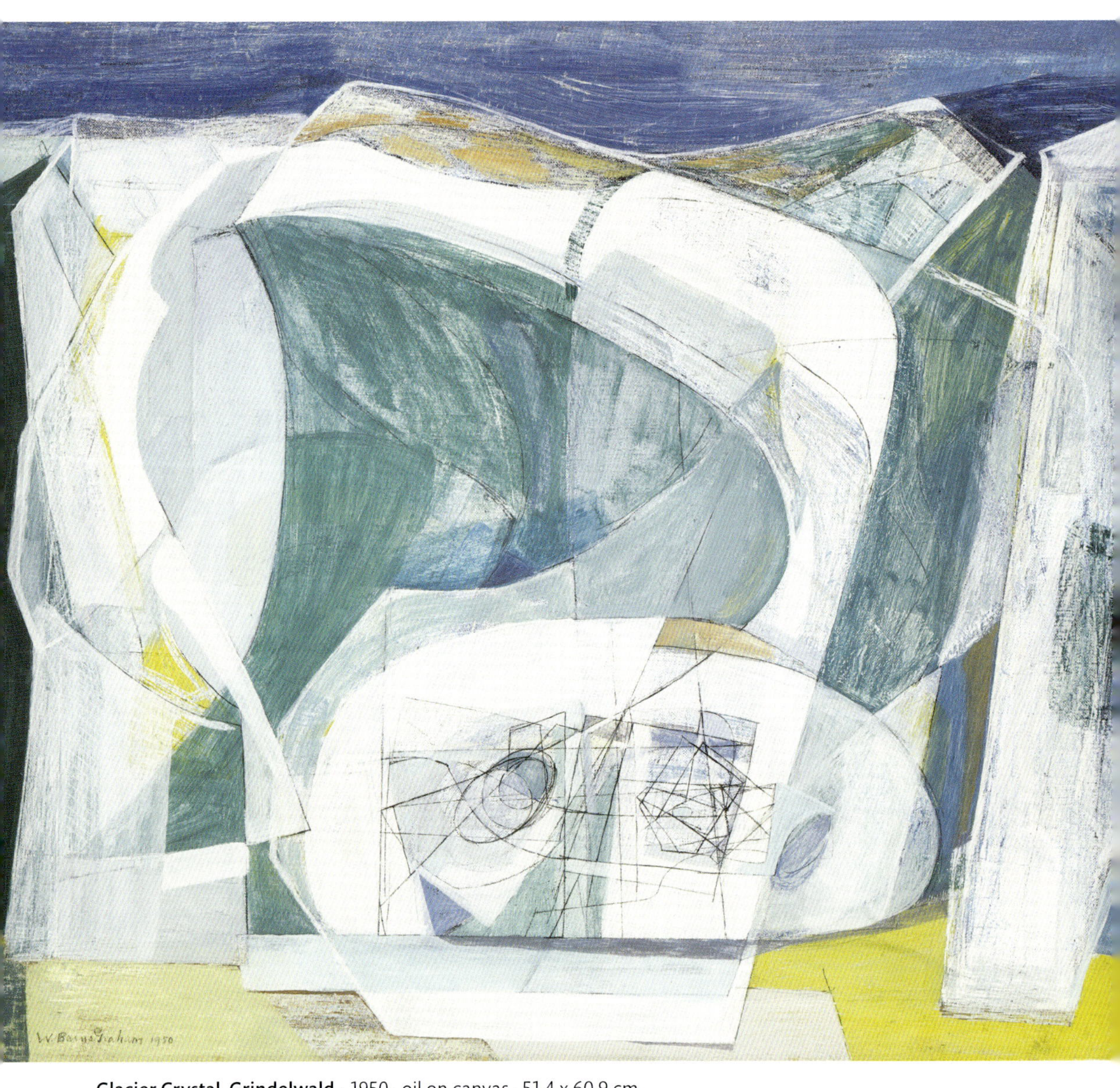

Glacier Crystal, Grindelwald · 1950 · oil on canvas · 51.4 x 60.9 cm

Tate · presented by the Contemporary Art Society, 1964 · T00708 · photo © Tate

3 Abstraction a 'process of laying bare'[1]

By the mid-1950s Barns-Graham was regarded as one of Britain's leading abstract painters. This chapter considers the context of her breakthrough 'Glacier' series produced between 1949 and 1951 and assesses its importance in her oeuvre. The 'Glacier' subject resonated with a number of thematic and philosophical preoccupations within the 'St Ives' community of artists at that time, as they attempted collectively to reinvent modernist practice following the upheaval of war. For Barns-Graham it represented her serious engagement with the work of the leading senior avant-garde 'St Ives' artists — namely Gabo, Hepworth and Nicholson, all of whom she admired — and through over 30 paintings, additional drawings and offset prints, her first sustained attempt to translate her perceptions of the world through a sophisticated process of abstraction.

In January 1952 'Glacier' works were showcased in her first one-person exhibition in London at the Redfern Gallery. An admirer of her work, the prominent critic J.P. Hodin recommended a change of motif, warning that such obsessive attachment might impede her progress.[2] Hodin was way off the mark as her concentration on the theme laid the foundations for the evolution of her abstract language in the 1950s. The reception of the 'Glacier' works through critical interest, purchases and exhibitions proved that she was as capable as any of her peers of making a strong contemporary statement, indeed they exemplify 'St Ives' concerns at that time, as Michael Bird has commented of *Glacier Crystal, Grindelwald* (1950):

> *This work demonstrates, as elegantly as anything produced in St Ives around 1950, the fusion of the Constructivist spirit with a revival of landscape art for which the town was becoming known.*[3]

Having endured her father's lack of belief in her chosen career, with her 'Glacier' works on the walls of a Cork Street gallery Barns-Graham was able to consider herself established as a serious painter.

The pursuit of abstraction in the late 1940s was no guarantee of success, but it represented a set of beliefs about the world. The war had rendered the utopian idealism of the interwar years obsolete, forcing the avant-garde to rethink modernism. During the 1940s figurative styles of art (Neo-romanticism and Social Realism) had gained popularity while reactions to abstract art remained largely hostile. A protracted, heated debate about the relative merits of abstraction and realism crystallised in an exchange between the young critics Patrick Heron and John Berger (1926–2017) in the *New Statesman and Nation* and the *Listener* between 1951 and 1953, with Berger promoting realism as an art form for the Left, while Heron endorsed abstraction as an art form devoid of ideological constraints. Heron played a key role in positioning 'St Ives' during this period, arguing for a type of painting that steered between pure abstraction and representation, drawing on the 'lyrical synthesis' achieved by Georges Braque (1882–1963) and Pierre Bonnard (1867–1947). Scepticism about abstraction persisted; for example, in 1956 the Tate Gallery's Director John Rothenstein (1901–1992) condemned Nicholson's abstraction as 'a new academicism', informed by a 'shallow' philosophy.[4] But by the end of the decade, with a growing emphasis on individual creative freedom, and excitement aroused by American Abstract Expressionism, abstraction had prevailed.

Among the 'St Ives' artists, the development of abstraction centred on the theme of organic growth, resonating with wider concerns about post-war regeneration.[5] Drawing on the theories of D'Arcy Wentworth Thompson, Barns-Graham used the proportional system of the Golden Section to compose her 'Glacier' pictures. His widely read *On Growth and Form* (1917, reprinted in 1942) demonstrated how maths underpins morphogenesis, the process of natural growth determining the formation of patterns and structures in animals and plants.[6] *On Growth and Form* informed the theoretical writings of Herbert Read, who promoted the idea that abstract art should derive from natural rhythms and proportions, and offered artists a template for representing nature's regenerative impulses.[7] Thompson's account of organic growth, supported by diagrams, graphs, drawings and photographs, was a seminal influence that Barns-Graham internalised as part of her own world view.[8]

The 'Glacier' theme: 'a process of laying bare'
After the hiatus of war Barns-Graham was poised for a step-change in her work, and encouragement from Nicholson, Hepworth and Bernard Leach

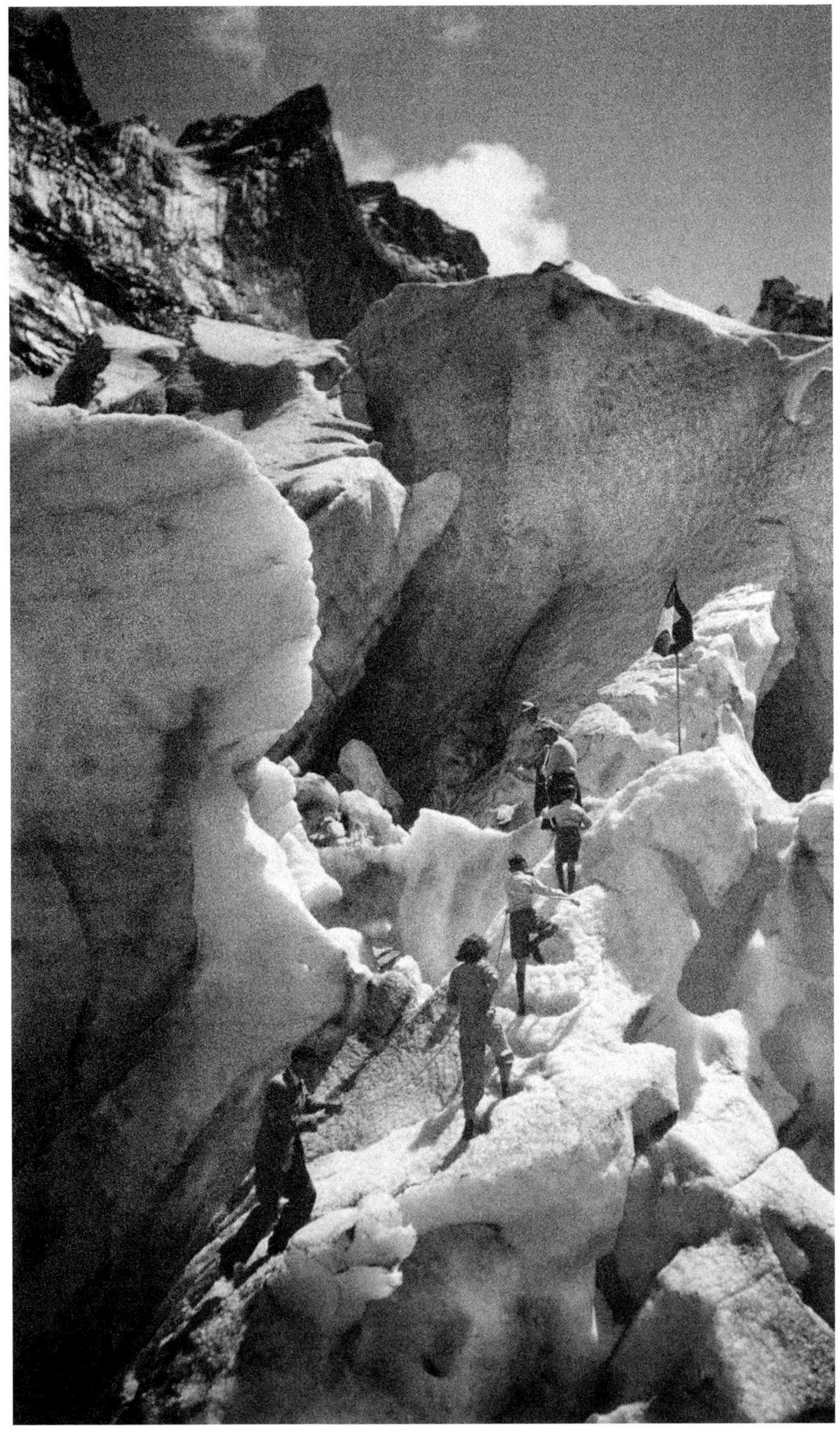

Barns-Graham with the Brotherton family on Grindelwald Glacier, 1949

bolstered her ambition. She wrote to her parents in 1947:

> *I don't think I'll look back from now — I know to go on: Seemingly I have*
> *every reason to provided I really work in the future — & that is where Barbara*
> *thinks I've lacked & its time I know myself I've not been confident inside enough*
> *— I know now that I evidently have something original to say & that I ought*
> *with work to get known.*[9]

In the late 1940s, along with Wells and Lanyon, she was influenced by Gabo
and Hepworth's explorations of the interior/exterior theme. *Box Factory Fire*
(pp. 24–25) shows her tackling this before May 1949 when she accompanied
the Brotherton family (friends she had met in St Ives) on a holiday to Switzerland
(below). Leaving behind tensions in St Ives — exacerbated by the newly-instigated
Penwith Society of Artists — and away from the shared currency of Cornish
landscape motifs, she was receptive to new subject matter. Under the North
Face of the Eiger she encountered the Grindelwald Glacier. Although Barns-
Graham only spent a day alone on the glacier, resulting in a few watercolours
and drawings, the effect was momentous. On her return to St Ives she synth-
esised her experience with various influences and ideas, working productively
in the studio.

The physical impact of the glacier on her senses had been overwhelming. The
contrast of its vast scale and intricately detailed crystalline formations served to

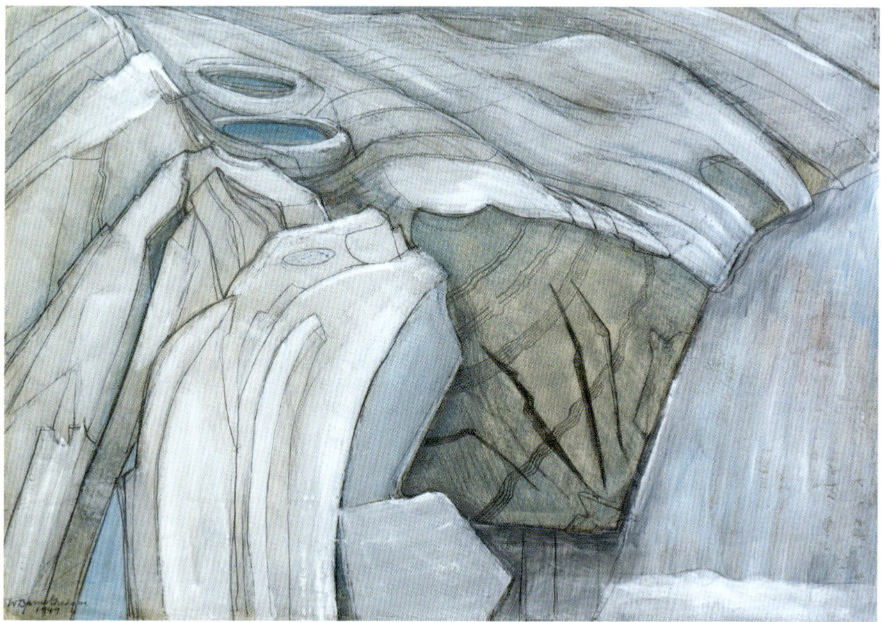

End of the Glacier Upper Grindelwald · 1949 · gouache and pencil on paper · 40 x 59 cm   BGT6399

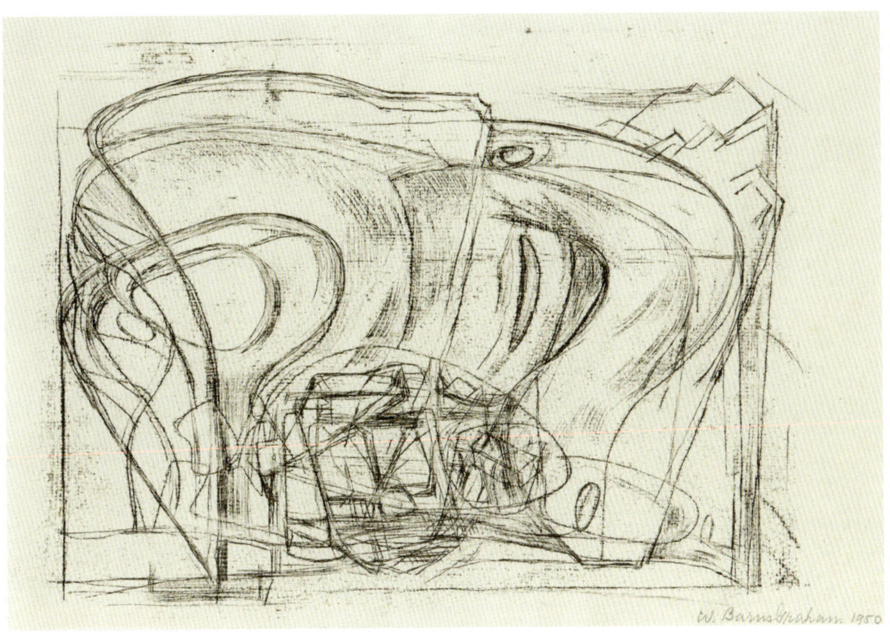

Upper Glacier Theme · 1950 · offset drawing on paper · 22.9 x 34.3 cm   BGT6003

emphasise a Cubist worldview in which perceptions of the world are experienced simultaneously, rather than from a fixed, single vantage point. She sensed the ice responding to climatic conditions — in a continual state of flux it was eroding the rock beneath as if it were a living, pulsating organism — and conveyed this abrasive action through incised lines, and by layering and scraping down paint.[10] Her palette of watery whites, cool blues, greys and greens, evokes a sense of place, but the translucency of ice also allowed her to reveal an ovoid structure buried in the glacier's core. In other images, especially offset prints and drawings, the outer layers of the glacier morph to resemble enlarged curved bones, or the gaping jaw of some prehistoric beast (*End of the Glacier Upper Grindelwald*, left). In a letter to the Tate Gallery in 1965 referring to *Glacier Crystal, Grindelwald* (1950), she recalled her experience:

> *At Grindelwald I was climbing on the two glaciers 'Upper' and 'Lower'.*
> *The massive strength and size of the glaciers, the fantastic shapes, the*
> *contrast of solidity and transparency, the many reflected colours in strong*
> *light, the warmth of the sun melting and changing the forms, in a few days*
> *a thinness could become a hole ... a piece could disintegrate and fall off,*
> *breaking the silence with a sharp crack and its echoes. It seemed to Breathe!*
> *Enormous standing forms, polished like glass with sharp edges ... which could*
> *include buried in it and on it, huge and tiny stones and rubble. This likeness*
> *to glass and transparency, combined in a work all angles at once, from*
> *above, through, and all round, as a bird flies, a total experience.*[11]

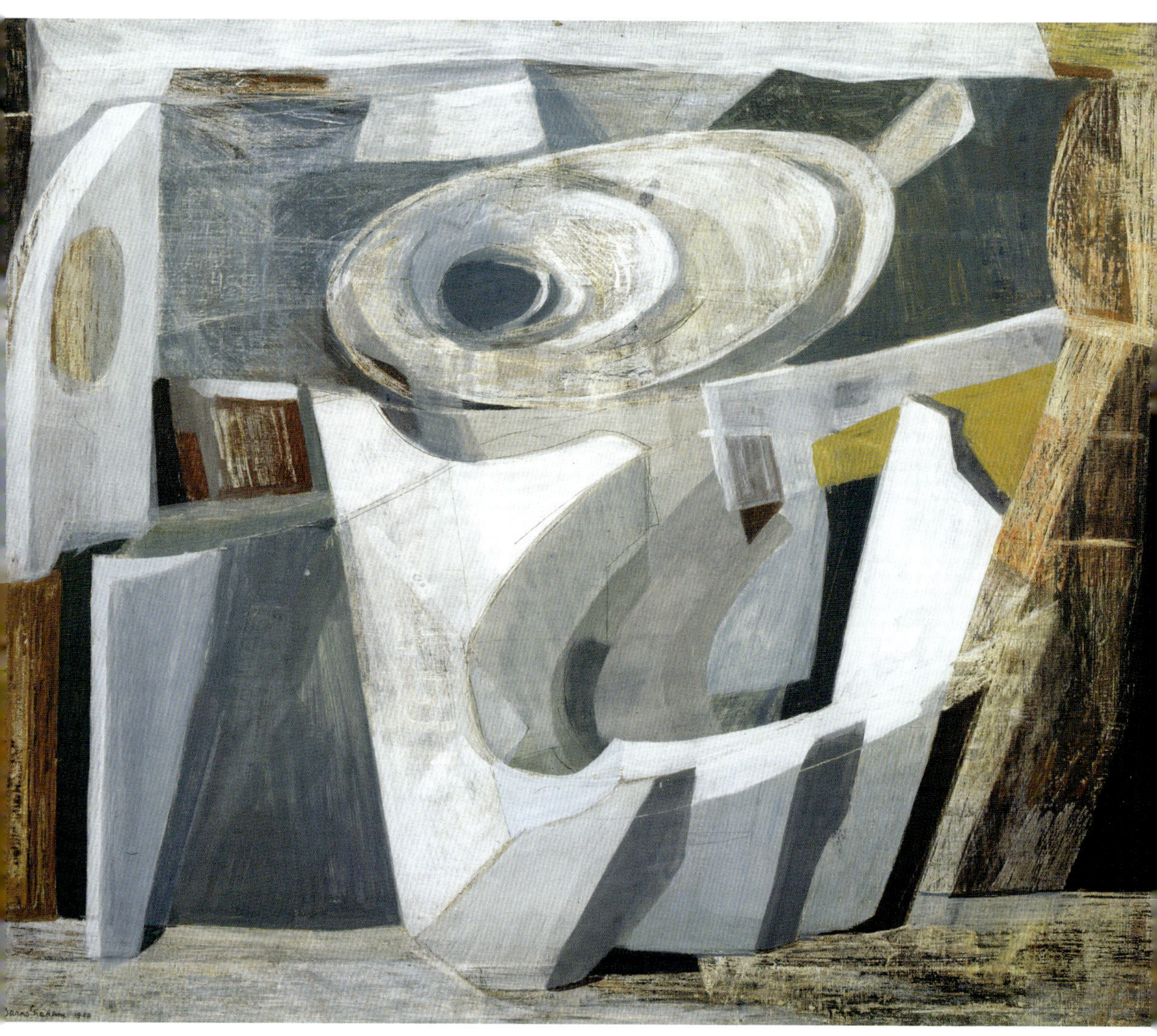

Glacier Vortex · 1950 · oil on canvas · 60 x 71.5 cm
Southampton City Art Gallery · bequeathed by Dr David and Liza Brown 2002

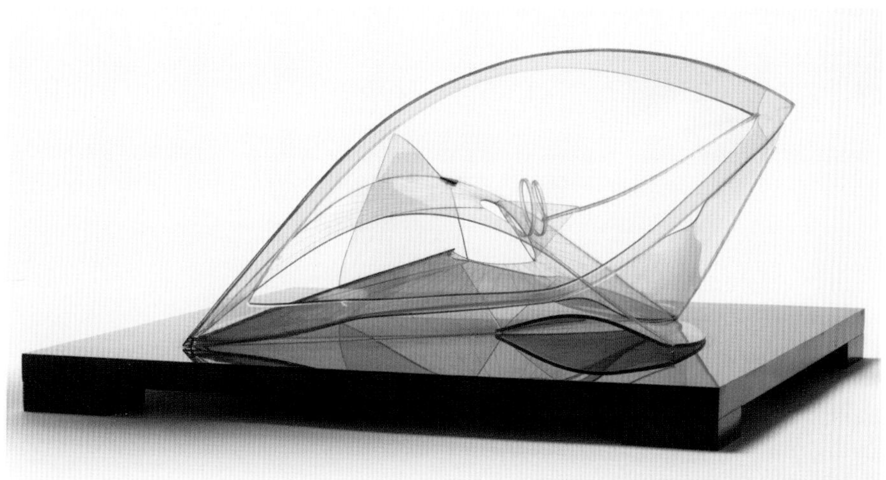

Naum Gabo · Spiral Theme · 1941 · cellulose acetate and perspex · 14 x 24.4 x 24.4 cm
Tate · presented by Miss Madge Pulsford 1958 · T00190 · photo © Tate · © The Work of Naum Gabo · © Nina and Graham Williams

Barns-Graham knew Naum Gabo during the war, and her use of his phrase 'as a bird flies, a total experience' indicates an affinity with his ideas. Educated in natural sciences as well as philosophy and art history, Gabo had been an advocate of Constructivism since the 1920s. He was convinced that to reflect reality art should incorporate the experience of space and time and he pursued this idea, making constructions in Perspex, a new transparent material that enabled him to emphasise volume as space rather than as solid mass. Before Gabo left for the United States in 1946 Barns-Graham acquired a smaller version of his construction *Spiral Theme* (above). Its layers of transparent forms suggest the unfolding of growth over time, its interior energy determining the exterior form.[12]

Explaining Gabo's Constructivism in 1948, Read noted that while his understanding of reality derived from modern science, his creative construction was poetic: 'It is the poetry of space, the poetry of time, of universal harmony, of physical unity.'[13] In the 'Glacier' works, Barns-Graham can be seen exploring the relationship between the internal forces of the ice-sheet shaping its appearance, referencing the dynamic curves of works by Gabo that were familiar to her.[14] In short, she perceived the three-dimensional structure of the Glacier in sculptural terms. Her achievement was to imaginatively translate this idea into two-dimensional pictorial space, using the Golden Section and such painterly means as colour and texture, to infuse her work with a lyrical and emotional intensity (eg. *Glacier Vortex*, left).

Hepworth was also adapting Constructivist principles and the interior/exterior theme in her sculptures of this period. Contemporaries would have recognised Barns-Graham's visual quotation of such works as *Oval Sculpture* (overleaf), or

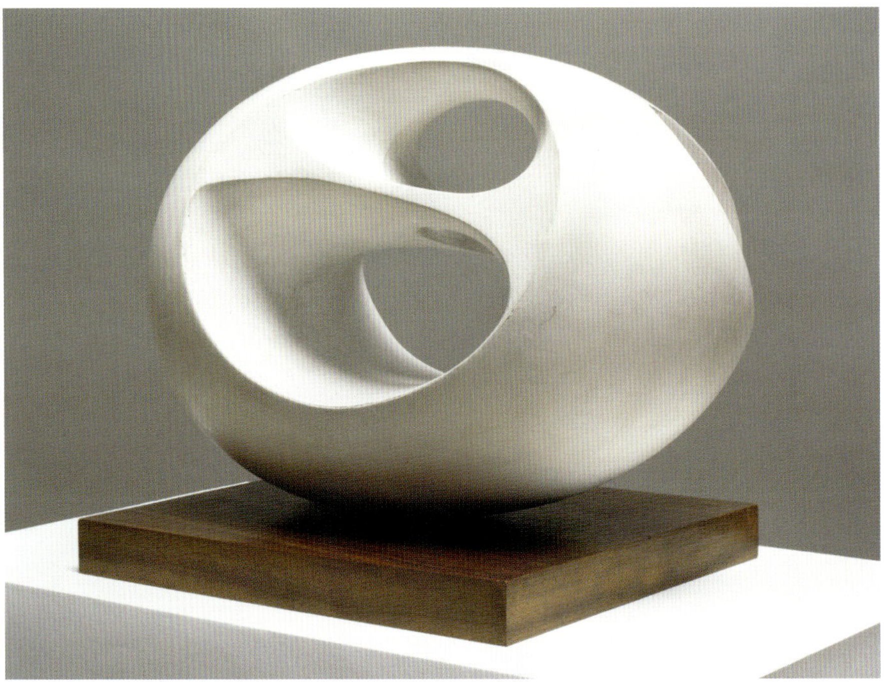

Barbara Hepworth · Oval Sculpture (No. 2)
1943 (cast 1958) · plaster on wooden base · 29.3 x 40 x 25.5 cm

the later, cave-like *Pendour* (1947—8). In such works Hepworth set out to express the physical and psychological feeling of being in the landscape, enveloped by its protective embrace. Barns-Graham extended this concept of landscape into painting, translating her apprehension of the massive ice-sheet as a sublime, awe-inspiring force of great beauty and calmness.

Ideas of immersion in landscape were gaining currency in the early 1950s through, for example, Jacquetta Hawkes's bestselling, quasi-archaeological book *A Land* (1951), in which the author declared her use of the sciences of geology and archaeology 'for purposes altogether unscientific'. Through a four-billion year history of the Earth she stressed the interconnectedness of human life with nature, drawing on poetic imagination, memory and feeling through the body as valid ways of knowing.[15]

Working on the 'Glacier' theme across different media supported the emergence of Barns-Graham's own abstract vocabulary, particularly through the process of offset or carbon transfer drawing, a variant of monotype printing developed by Klee and disseminated by his colleague Jankel Adler (1895–1949), whom she met in Glasgow through Colquhoun and MacBryde. Colquhoun was a skilled practitioner of offset drawing and Barns-Graham picked up useful techniques

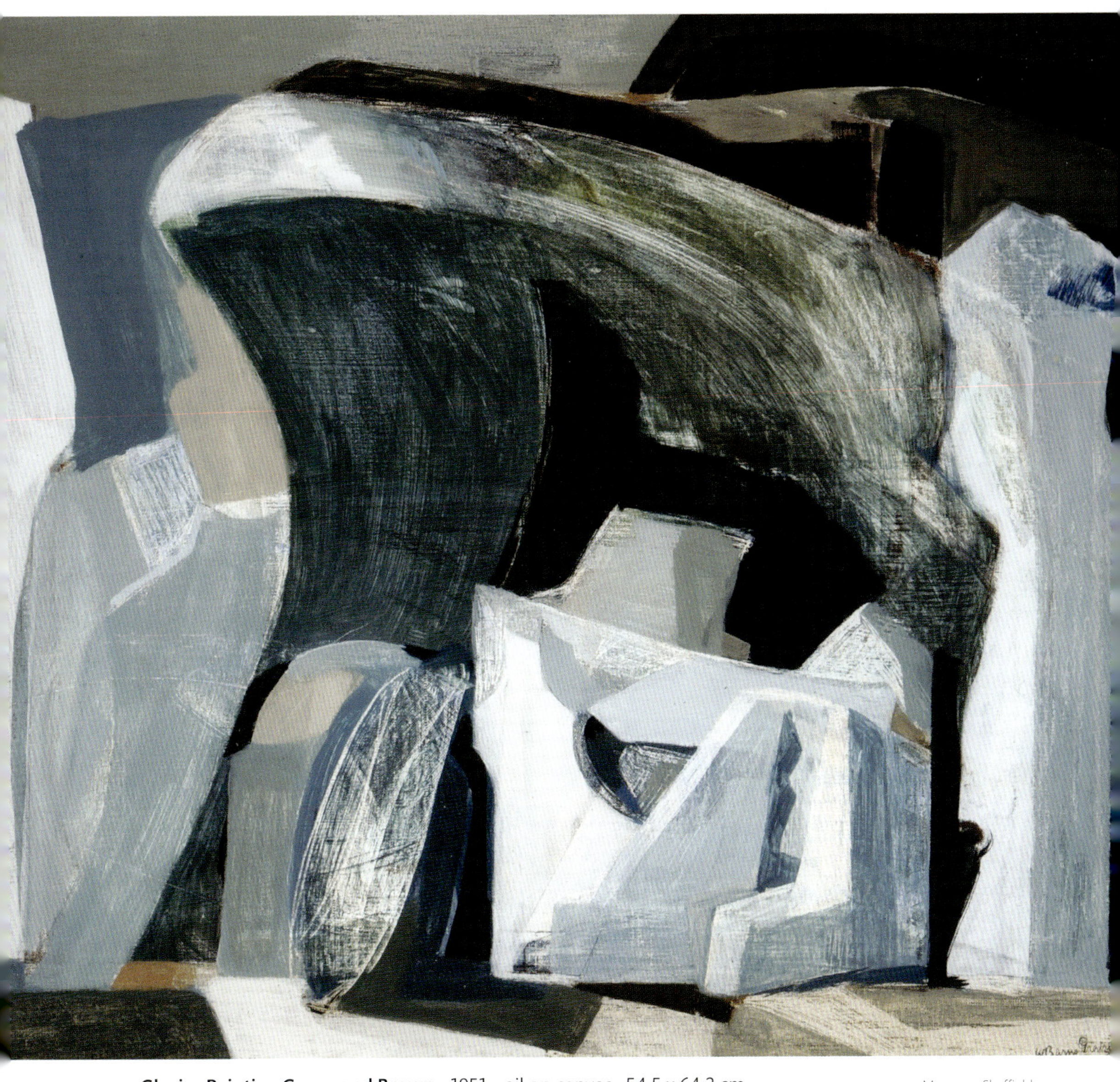

Glacier Painting Green and Brown · 1951 · oil on canvas · 54.5 x 64.2 cm   Museums Sheffield

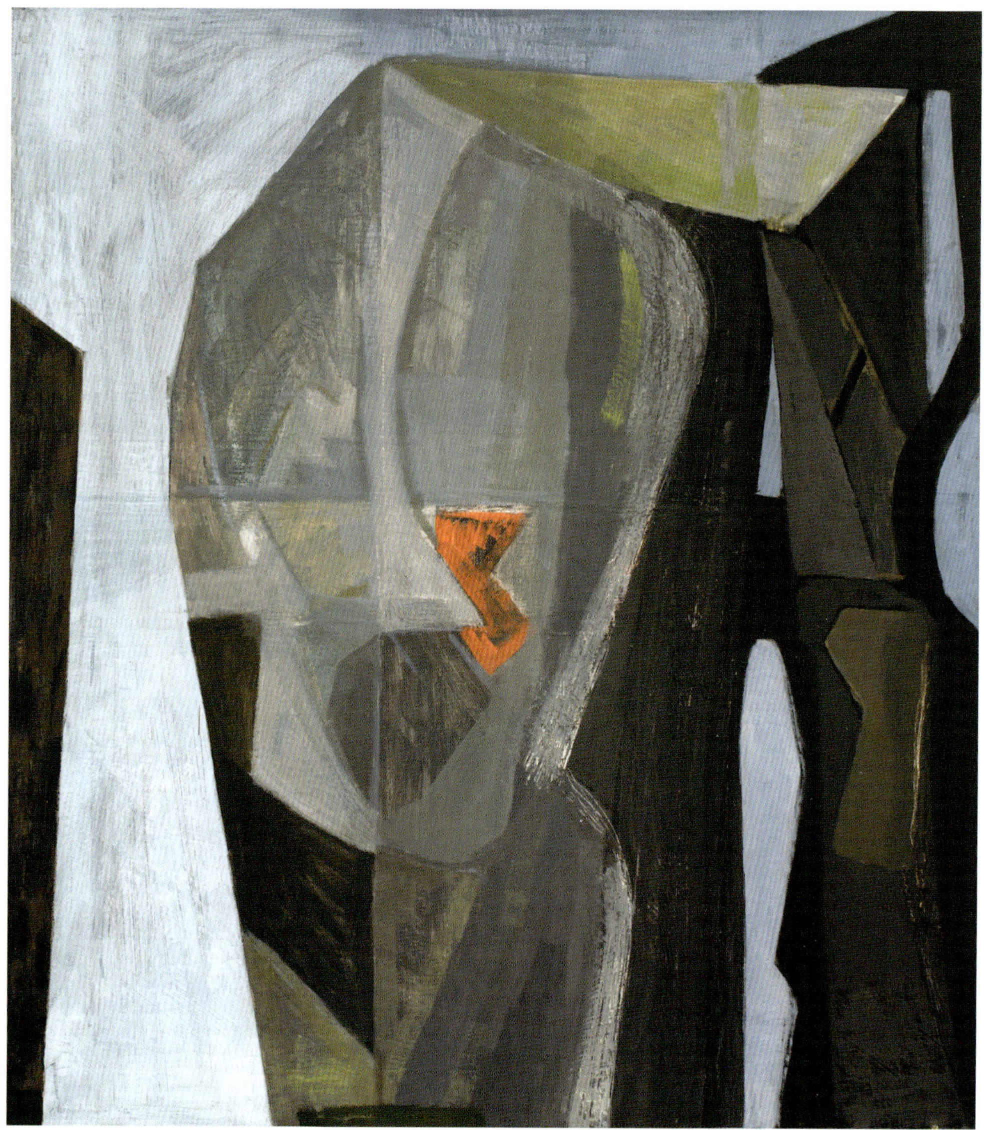

Cliff Face · 1952 · oil on canvas · 102.8 x 92.7 cm BGT385

from him.[16] The process involves tracing a preparatory drawing onto another sheet, with a third sheet coated in ink or oil paint functioning as a carbon paper. A sharp instrument such as a scriber (Barns-Graham also used a knitting needle or nail) is then traced over the original drawing, offsetting it on to the underlying sheet.[17] With its speed, chance marks, blurry lines and smudgy, uneven textures, offset drawing allowed fluency in working through an idea. In 1950, assessing the 'Glacier' works in his essay 'Cornish Renaissance' for the widely read *Penguin New Writing*, J.P. Hodin noted the positive effect of this process on her work:

> *... she has reached not only a material beauty — a kind of offset technique, developed by Paul Klee — but also a musical beauty through abstract forms derived from [the experience].*[18]

Using a variety of mark-making to interrogate her subject — from controlled, linear distillation to fluid, translucent or opaque brushwork — introduced a new way of working that encouraged her to try out different effects. The technique of scraping back a painted surface had been favoured by Nicholson since the 1920s, and widely adopted by the younger generation of artists; it became synonymous with 'St Ives' style. The abrasive treatment of the support, whether canvas, board or paper, paralleled Barns-Graham's perceptions of natural processes of attrition while drawing attention to the physical properties of the painting as an object.

In 1949 she told Hodin that she liked 'to see nature in motion working on and changing itself', and while engaged with the 'Glacier' theme she began a related series based on rock forms shaped by the movement of ice, water and the earth's crust.[19] In *Glacier Painting Green and Brown* (p. 59), for example, the 'Glacier' and 'Rock Form' themes seem to merge.

These geomorphological aspects of landscape provided motifs that could be deployed in different ways to produce arrangements of simplified abstract forms. For Barns-Graham the role of the artist was not to invent reality, but to reveal it through the language of abstraction, through a process of stripping back, 'a process of laying bare', as she explained to Hodin in 1949:

> *... though I seldom do a purely abstract painting: I am interested in using abstract forms mainly insofar as they are derived directly from natural sources by means of simplification within the movement of the picture itself: painting is pattern, and paintings should be just as good upside down, sideways, in a looking glass: I use a looking [glass] constantly in painting, and often turn my compositions upside down and on end when I am working.*[20]

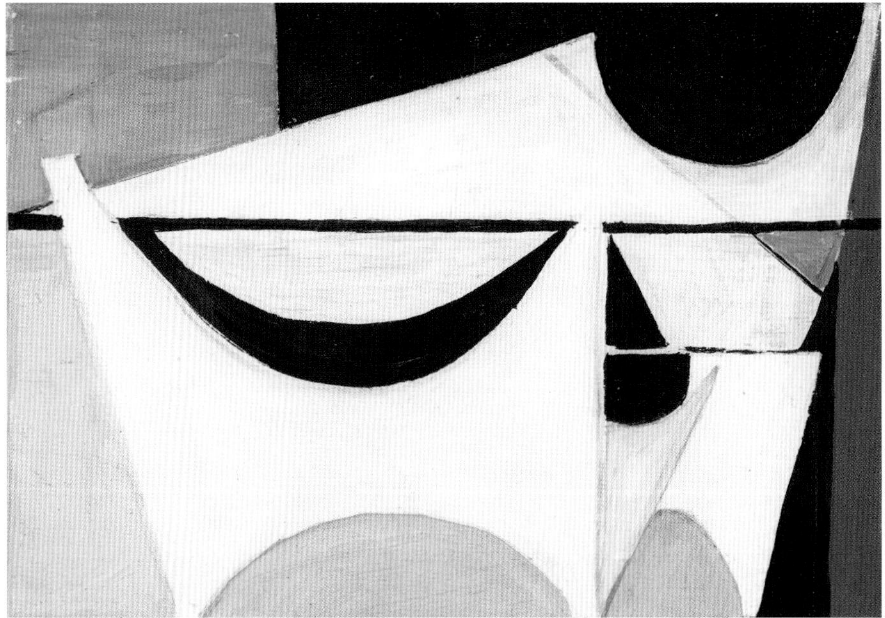

White Relief On Black and Grey · 1954 · oil and hardboard relief · 13.9 x 20.4 cm

Translating perceptions: the legacy of Cubism

With Nicholson, and others at this time, Barns-Graham looked to the legacy of Cubism as a philosophy and method for representing perceived reality. In 1948 she acquired a new English translation of Daniel-Henry Kahnweiler's monograph on the Cubist artist Juan Gris (1887–1927). Rachel Rose Smith has noted her bookmark at the page where the 'analytic' phase of Cubism is explained as a recreation of experience through the presentation of multiple viewpoints.[21] This strategy is clearly at work in Barns-Graham's two still-life compositions based on a horse's skull of 1951 and 1952, in which the solid skull is disassembled on the picture plane from multiple perspectives (eg. *Green Skull Form I*, right).

Crucially, Cubism provided the means of dispensing with pictorial illusion and asserting the reality of the picture surface. In the 'Glacier' and 'Rock Form' series, it enabled her to increasingly abstract forms from nature, resulting in several large, almost monochrome paintings. In *Composition (Sea)* (overleaf) a horizon line and scratchy textured surface suggest a coastal landscape, but the painting's mostly hard-edged, abutting geometric shapes offer an equivalent to the real world rather than a description. These ambitious canvases evidence her determination to build on the success of the 'Glacier' works, as did a subsequent series of small three-dimensional carved reliefs in which her abstract forms exist in real space.

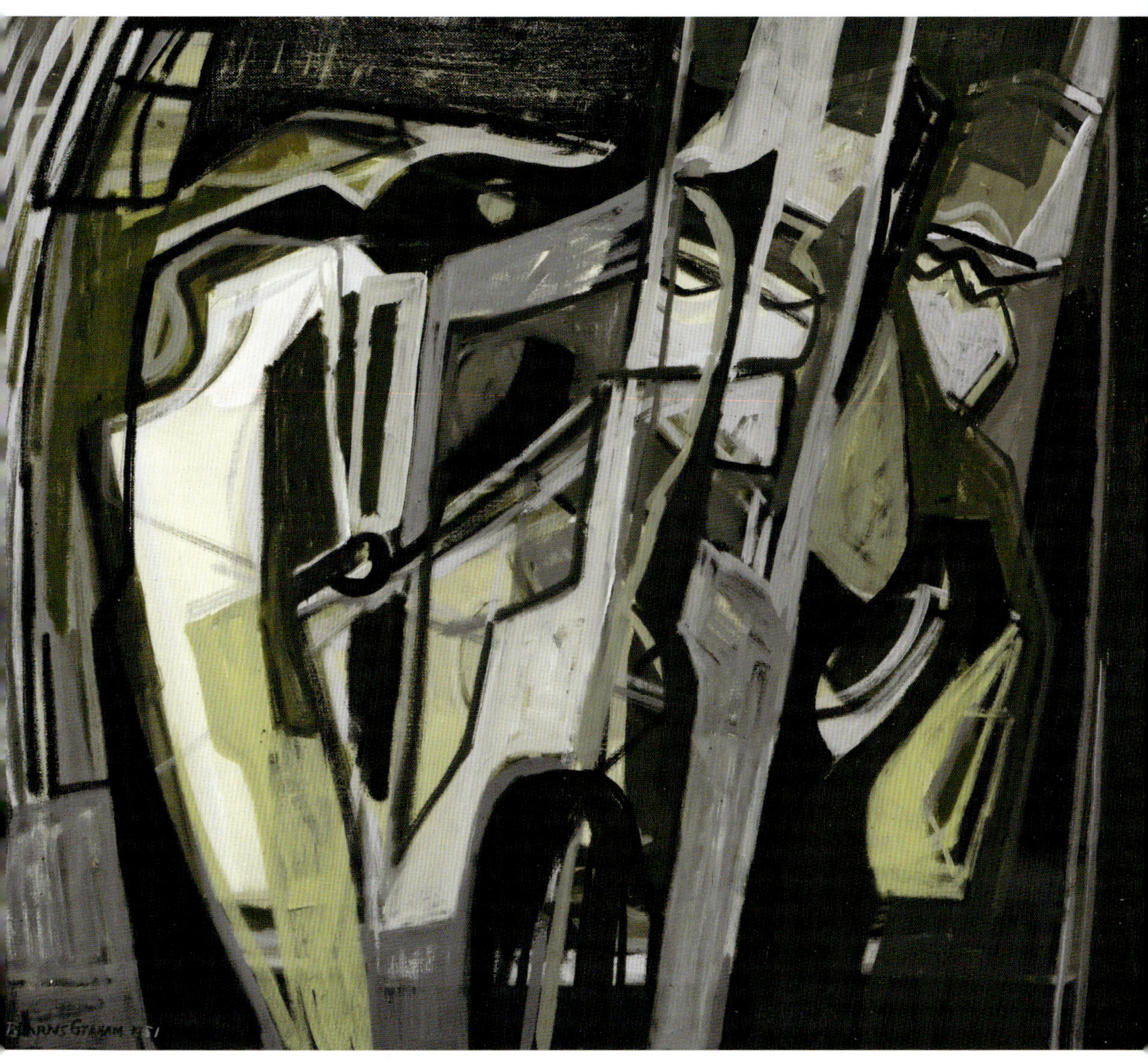

Green Skull Form I · 1951 · oil on canvas · 50.5 x 60.6 cm
The Hepworth Wakefield · presented by Wilhelmina Barns-Graham Trust 2019

overleaf · **Composition (Sea)** · 1954 · oil on canvas · 45.5 x 76 cm · BGT6407

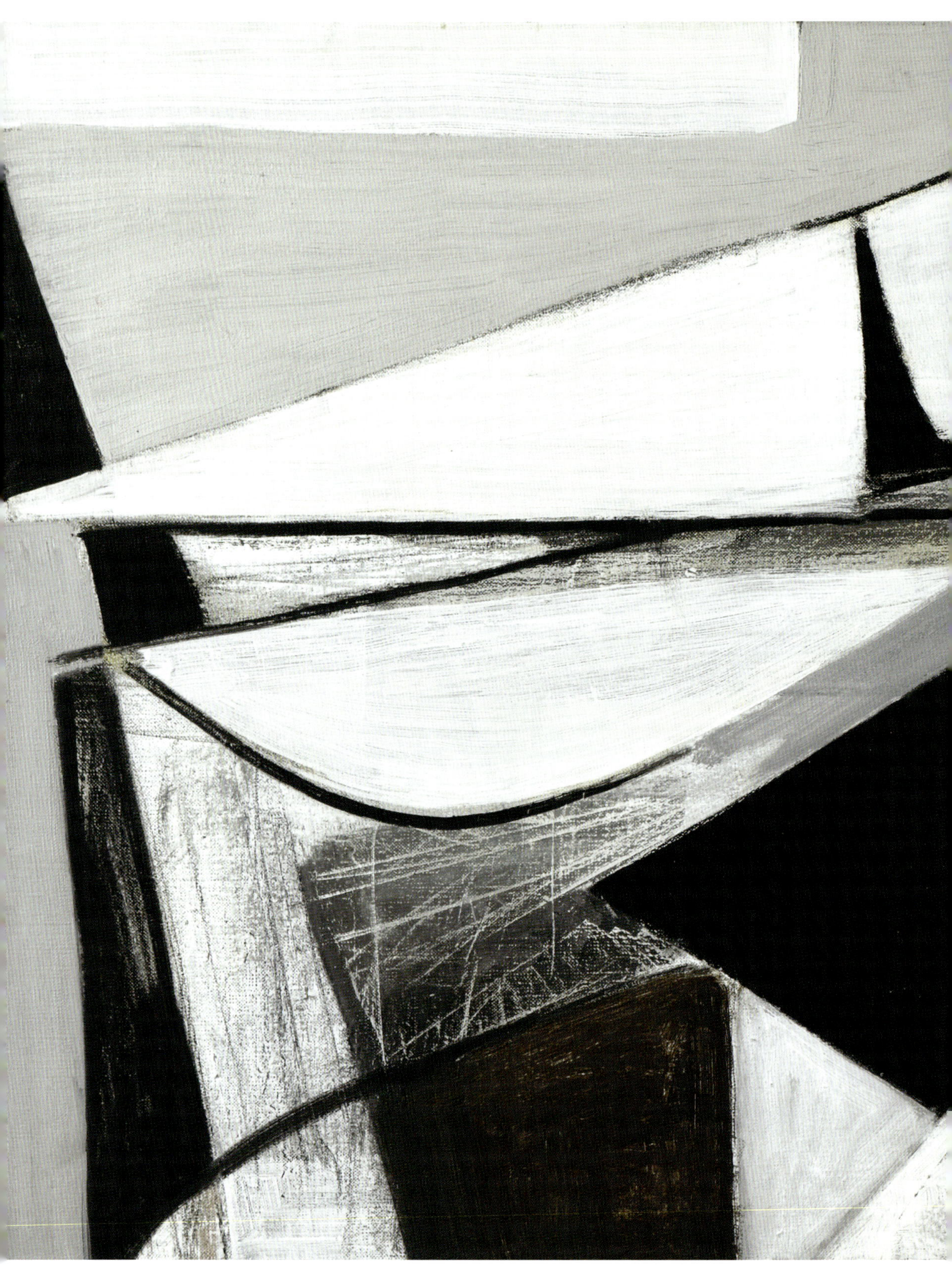

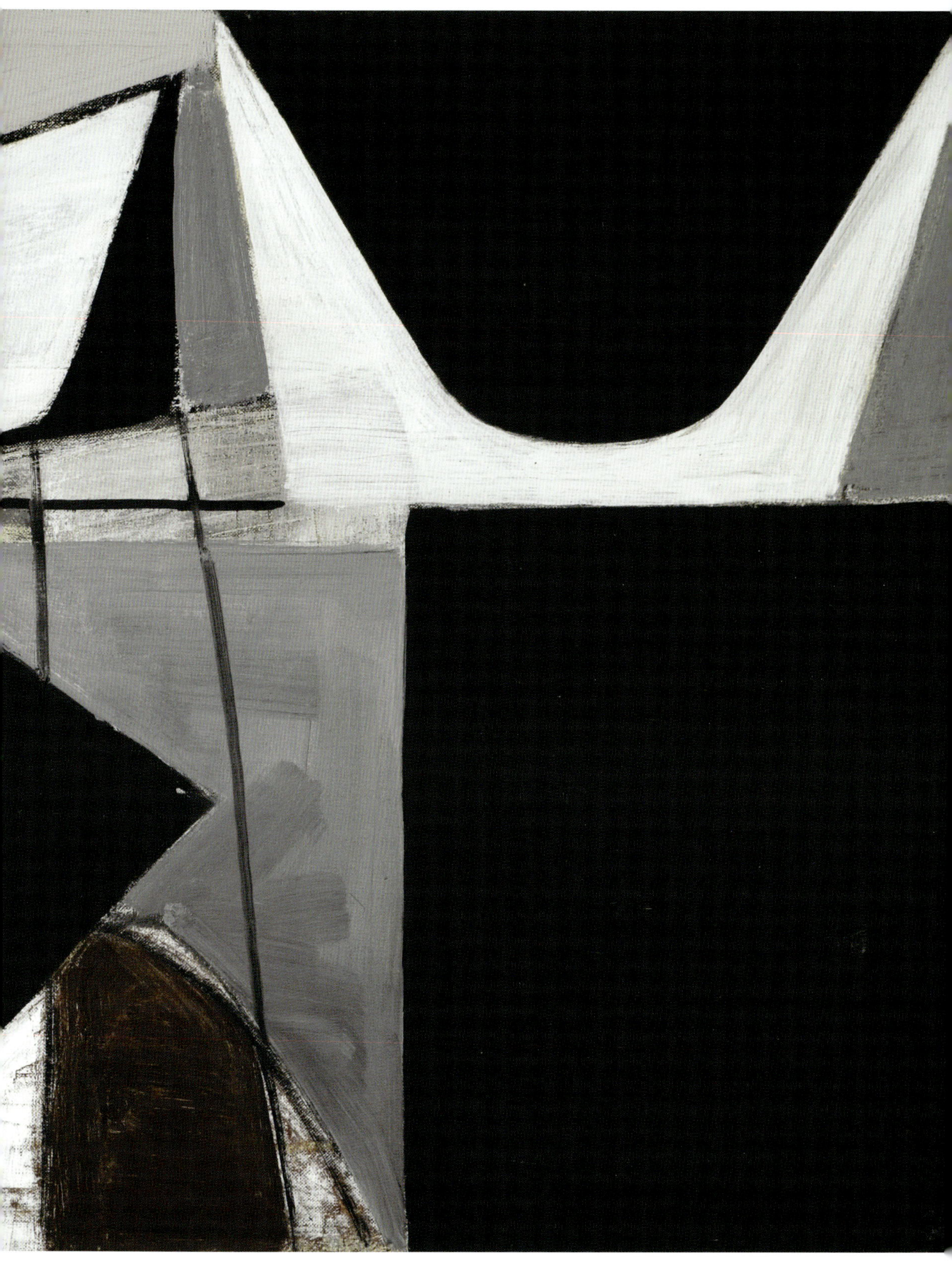

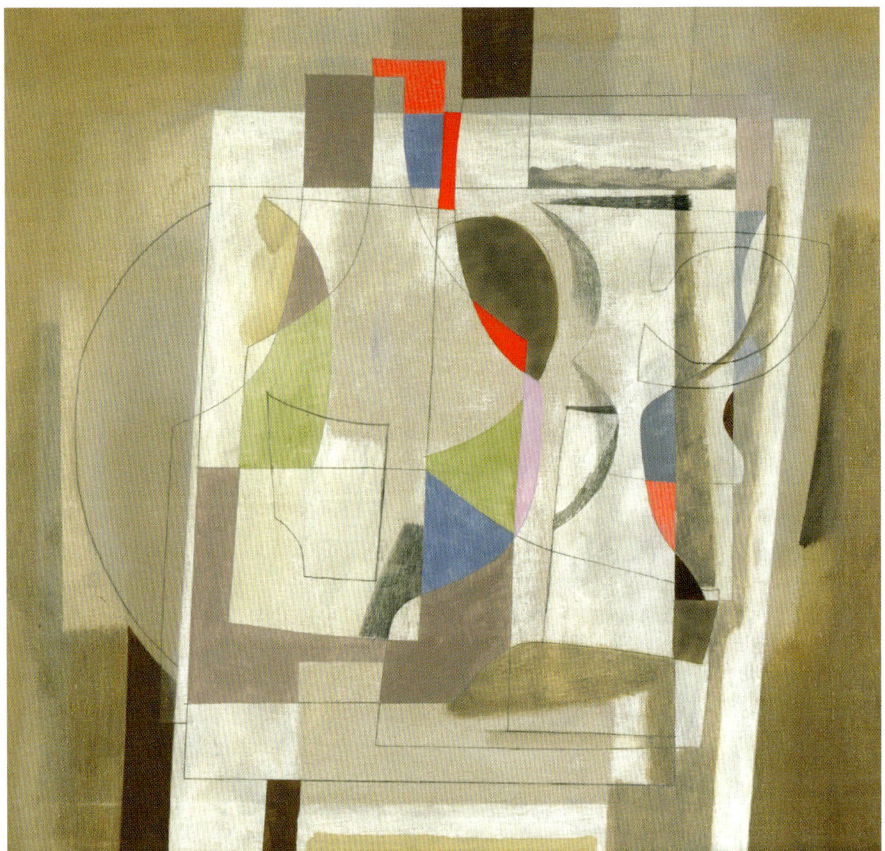

Ben Nicholson · **Feb 2-54** · 1954 · oil paint and graphite on canvas · 73.3 x 80.3 cm

Nicholson had of course pioneered the use of reliefs, and as Lynne Green has noted, some of Barns-Graham's 'Rock Form' paintings also resemble the Cubist-inspired, table-top still life format favoured by Nicholson.[22] Importantly for Barns-Graham and other 'St Ives' artists, Nicholson's reworking of pre-war Cubism through these acclaimed still-life paintings illustrated how a modernist idiom could be successfully united with aspects of naturalism. In the post-war period, this middle ground no doubt helped to validate Barns-Graham's own position, which was to derive her abstraction from the world of experience.

Her paring down of landscape forms and investigation of nature's invisible, internal structures and forces became both a subject and method of working that defined her output in this period, establishing her reputation. Even later, at its most severely abstract, her work would be underpinned by a desire to convey a human connection to unseen rhythms and forces, an approach that began with the 'Glacier' theme.[23] She owned a 1951 edition of Herbert Read's *The Meaning of Art* (1931), which contains a cautionary note to artists pursuing pure abstraction that justified her preferred way of working:

> *Abstract art ... like realistic art, is always in danger of degenerating into academicism ... It fails to renew its forces at the source of all forms, which is not so much nature as the vital impulses which determine the evolution of life itself. For that reason alone it may be suggested that an alternation between abstraction and realism is desirable in any artist.*[24]

Although Barns-Graham revisited the 'Glacier' theme in the 1970s and 1980s, she felt that art-historical fascination with her initial 'Glacier' works had distracted attention from subsequent developments in her oeuvre. But in their response to nature as a living entity, the 'Glacier' paintings are perhaps even more significant today. In light of the current human-induced and seemingly inexorable retreat of the world's glaciers and melting icecaps, they shine brightly as poignant reminders of nature as a living organism, and of our place within it.

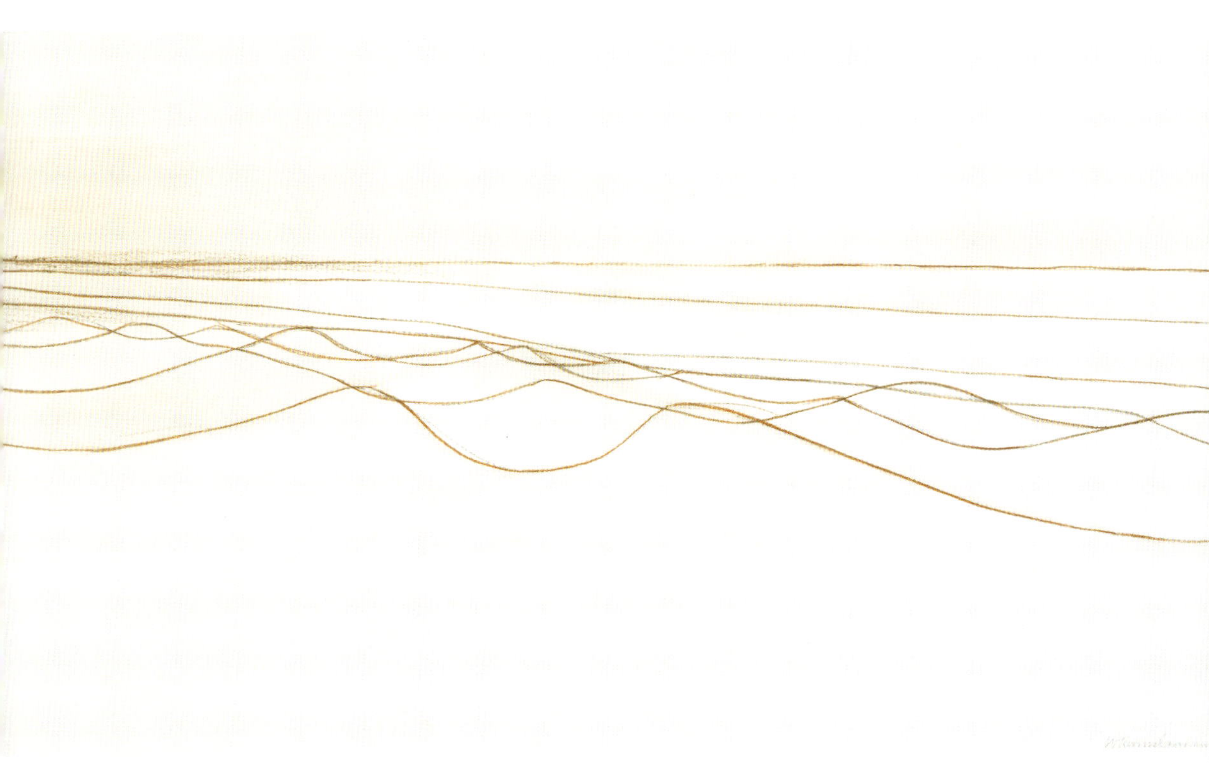

Eight Lines, Porthmeor · 1986 · chalk on paper · 34.5 x 62.7 cm

4 **Drawing**
'a discipline of the mind'

Drawing is another side to oneself. It's not my main work; my main work is my abstract – or abstraction – paintings, colour, texture. But I believe in drawing and I've always drawn.[1]

Although Barns-Graham regarded drawing as less important than her painting, it clearly occupied a special place in her practice. Her facility as a draughtswoman and the distinctive, architectural quality of her line was admired throughout her career, though her drawing style varied in response to different subjects, and to meet different ends. As Mel Gooding has noted:

Her drawing is a wonderfully flexible instrument, always alive to the dynamism and rhythm of things, whether in lightly annotating the repetition of a wave, exploring the underlying structure of a hill or coastal landscape, or registering the monumental mass and magical translucency of a glacier.[2]

Through a process of intense observation and versatile mark-making, Barns-Graham used drawing to extract forms from nature. She constantly turned to drawing as a way of seeing, discovering, thinking and understanding, of honing and translating her 'inner perception' of underlying external realities. She enjoyed the peculiar perceptual concentration that takes hold during the act of drawing, as described by Tania Kovats:

The mental state when making drawings is most commonly one of total absorption, a withdrawing and removal of attention from anything other than the drawing; the sense of draw meaning to extract. The world is reduced to the piece of paper and becomes a repository for thought, speculation, observation and projection.[3]

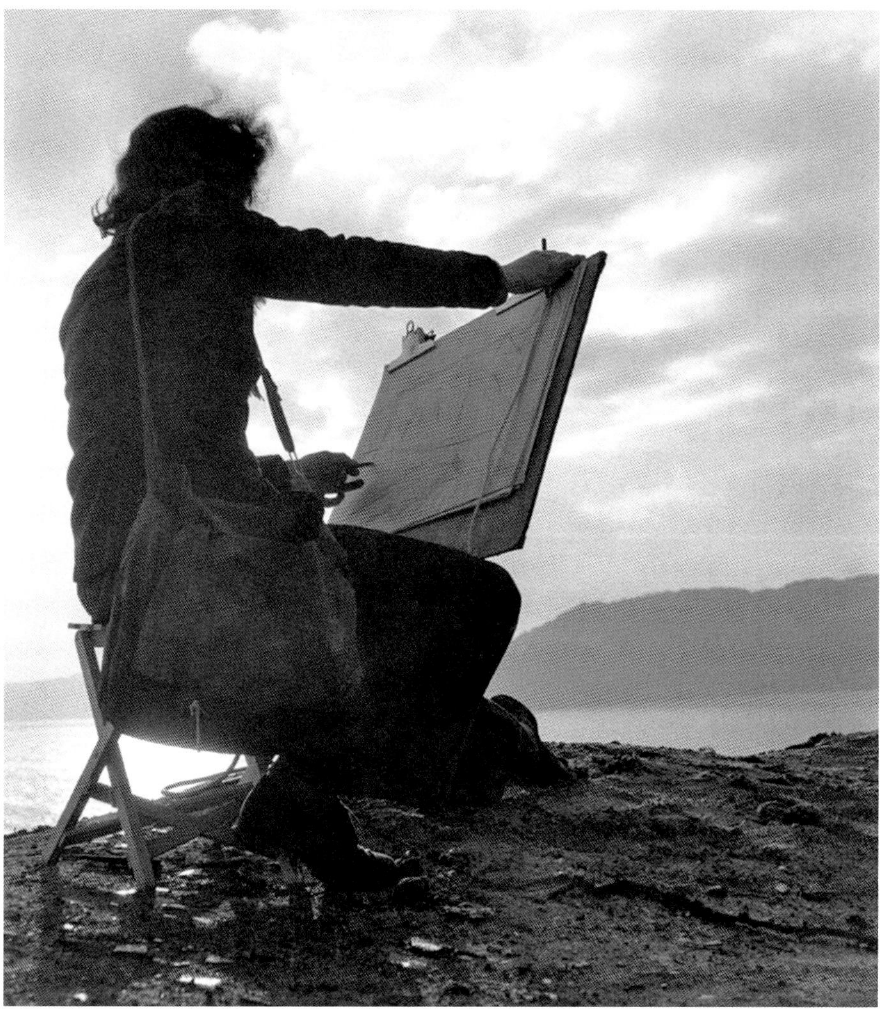

Barns-Graham sketching from a vantage point above Porthgwidden, St Ives, 1947
Central Office of Information

Drawing was pivotal to the development of Barns-Graham's painting and to her identity as an artist. Her physical, conceptual and emotional engagement with nature through drawing was profound. From the 1960s onwards she made numerous line drawings of the sand and sea in motion based on mathematical calculations that relate to her series of 'Expanding Forms'. But she also turned her back to the beach in order to recompose its lines and rhythms from recollected sensation and memory.[4] Barns-Graham's drawings and etchings of waves continue to inform drawing students today, through works such as *Eight Lines, Porthmeor* (p. 68), in which she elegantly conveys the movement and volume of water rolling towards the coast and the impact of this on all her senses; a series of lines pulsate across the page, their rhythms echoing the sound of water meeting the shore.

The essence of things

As a student at Edinburgh College of Art — where drawing was considered
to be the foundation of artistic achievement — Barns-Graham was thoroughly
trained in observational drawing techniques. This early grounding informed all
aspects of her practice, representational or abstract.[5] Throughout the 1950s and
alongside her evolving abstract painting, she continued to make representational
drawings resulting from total immersion in landscape environments (eg. pictured,
left). The co-existence of these apparently contradictory approaches in her
work was unproblematic for Barns-Graham and, unlike many of her peers, she
exhibited both styles. After about 1950 her naturalistic drawings seem to relate
less directly, if at all, to her paintings, but observational drawing nevertheless
remained integral to the development of her abstract idiom. Her drawings were
not preparatory studies in a conventional sense, but they were indispensable
to the formulation of her unique vision since the synchronisation of eye and
hand allowed her to discover forms and shapes that would then emerge in
her paintings, as she later explained:

> *I have always been interested in drawing — it is a discipline of the mind.
> I seek to discover abstract shapes, accepting the subject's demands often
> touching different moods. I have sessions of drawing and consider it important
> to make studies, to develop one's awareness to inner perception, collecting
> shapes that become my shapes. To see later what is useful, now with increased
> understanding of the importance to be in union with nature. To identify oneself
> with its rhythm so that again, later, I can express myself in my own language.*[6]

Barns-Graham and other 'St Ives' artists understood that seeing is an active
process, in which perception of the outer world is filtered through individual
subjectivity and feeling, that the artist is in the world, not somehow looking
at it from an external position. Martin Kemp has argued that through the act
of drawing Barns-Graham's combination of 'inner seeing' and 'outer sensing'
allowed her over time to develop a heightened perception of natural forms.[7]
She recognised herself that the discipline of drawing facilitated this perceptual
and conceptual process, affording her greater freedom in her painting:

> *I seldom work from my drawings. The discipline used releases me in my
> paintings to work more freely, expand with ideas and imagination involving
> joy in colour, texture and harmony, I start creating.*[8]

As noted in the previous chapter, Barns-Graham's interpretation of the natural
world was framed by D'Arcy Wentworth Thompson's theories of natural
growth, which encouraged her through drawing to study its 'function of forms
and formations'. So the act of drawing was not only pleasurable, it represented

primary, phenomenological research into nature's internal dynamics: 'I get at the real essence of things which can be as miraculous as anything devised by imagination — as in the drama of the sea, the sky can astonish the mind.'[9] In his essay on Barns-Graham's drawings Gooding has noted that Gabo's use of line and drawing was particularly instructive for Barns-Graham as a means of seeing nature, of imagining its internal structures and forces. Gabo too acknowledged the mysterious fusion of the artist's imagination with external perception.[10] Leonardo Da Vinci's (1452–1519) investigative drawings that reveal such patterns in nature as the recurring spiral form in plants and gathering storms, were also influential. Da Vinci's penetrating insights offered proof that the subjective artist's eye could reveal objective scientific truths.

Barns-Graham liked to use mathematical grids as the basis for her drawings, seeking out the 'sculptural, architectural and linear qualities' of her chosen subject in order to understand and simplify its forms and movements.[11] But she altered her mark-making style in response to her subject as her studies of rocks in Formentera (right) clearly demonstrate. The expressive or metaphoric potential of the formal elements of drawing were also deployed in her abstract paintings. For example, in the 'Geoff and Scruffy' and 'Order and Disorder of Things of a Kind' series, which both centre on the relationships between things, she exploited the narrative connotations of drawing, as described by Paul Klee, whose work had been of interest to her since at least the mid-1930s. In his 'Creative Credo' first published in 1920, Klee described the dynamic and narrative possibilities of line, plane, and space — drawing's fundamental elements — explaining the relationships implied by each starting with the point or dot from which a line is drawn:

After a short time, we shall stop to catch our breath (the broken line, or the line articulated by several stops). I look back to see how far we have come (counter movement). Ponder the distance thus far travelled (sheaf lines). A river may obstruct our progress; we use a boat (wavy line). Further on there might be a bridge (series of curves). On the other bank we encounter someone who, like us, wishes to deepen his insight. At first we joyfully travel together (convergence), but gradually differences arise (two lines drawn independently of each other). Each party shows some excitement (expression, dynamism, emotional quality of the line).[12]

Drawing in the landscape: excursions and excavations

For most of her life Barns-Graham lived in rural settings surrounded by nature, which provided endless source material. The lifting of the wartime restrictions on outdoor sketching or painting meant that from the mid-1940s she was able

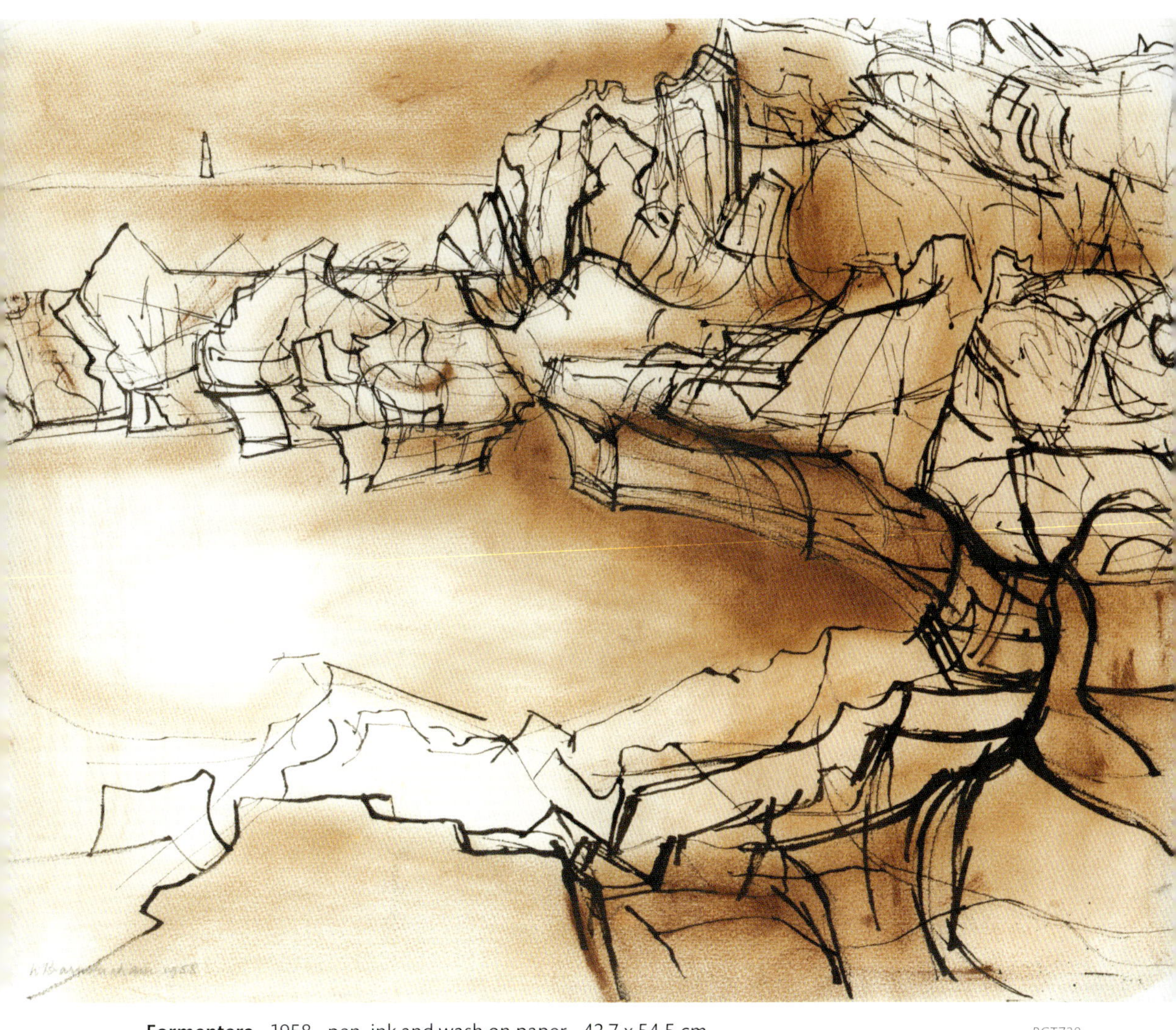

Formentera · 1958 · pen, ink and wash on paper · 42.7 x 54.5 cm

to make drawings in St Ives and the surrounding countryside. West Cornwall's peculiarly graphic landscape, with its fields delineated by hedges, was described by art critic Charles Marriott as 'a draughtsman's country' that lent itself to the abstract vision of an artist such as Ben Nicholson.[13] In 1949 Nicholson moved into Porthmeor Studios next to Barns-Graham. They often spent time in each other's studios, and in summer 1950 she accompanied him on several drawing excursions to Zennor, or along the coast. On these trips they both enjoyed reducing the landscape to carefully drawn arcs and lines.

In the 1950s Barns-Graham's trips away from Cornwall to other rural destinations were frequently taken on the recommendation of her doctor for recuperation. She was attracted to geomorphological landscapes, in which she could also recharge her work through drawing. In 1949, on her trip to the Swiss Bernese Alps she experienced the Grindelwald Glacier, and although she only made a few drawings in situ, she later developed the 'Glacier' theme through offset drawing and used drawn lines in her paintings to construct its crystalline forms. She also made several drawing trips to the Scilly Isles, the low lying archipelago twenty-eight miles off Land's End (notably in 1951 with her husband David Lewis and Nicholson), where she was struck by the curvilinear lines of land and sea (eg. *St Martins Lower Town I*, right).

During the 1950s, accompanied by Lewis she travelled extensively in Italy, exploring its varied landscapes and architecture through numerous large drawings made en plein air. On one such trip in 1954 they spent time in Venice, Florence and Chiusure in the Province of Siena. Despite the obvious attractions of Italy's Renaissance treasures, Lewis noted that it was the Italian landscape that captivated his wife:

> *Everywhere we went we tried to get out into the fields, into the sharp heat, and sudden shadows like dark ponds under the cypresses and figs. Willie made huge drawings — forty of them! Every day we started for the fields at 5 or half past five in the morning. Then Willie would begin drawing — would begin discovering with endless patience the structure of the landscape, the forms and tensions and rhythms of the hills.[14]*

The process of extracting her own forms and shapes from nature is clearly seen in a comparison of two pencil and tempera wash drawings, *Monte Olivetti, Tuscany* (p. 76) and *Clay Workings, Chiusure* (p. 77). In the former, curved, simplified lines describe a crevasse or ravine opening up in the foreground, while in the latter spatial perspective is virtually abandoned, the earthworks depicted by an upturned semi-circular curve and interlocking geometric forms. Curious about the effect of the elements on

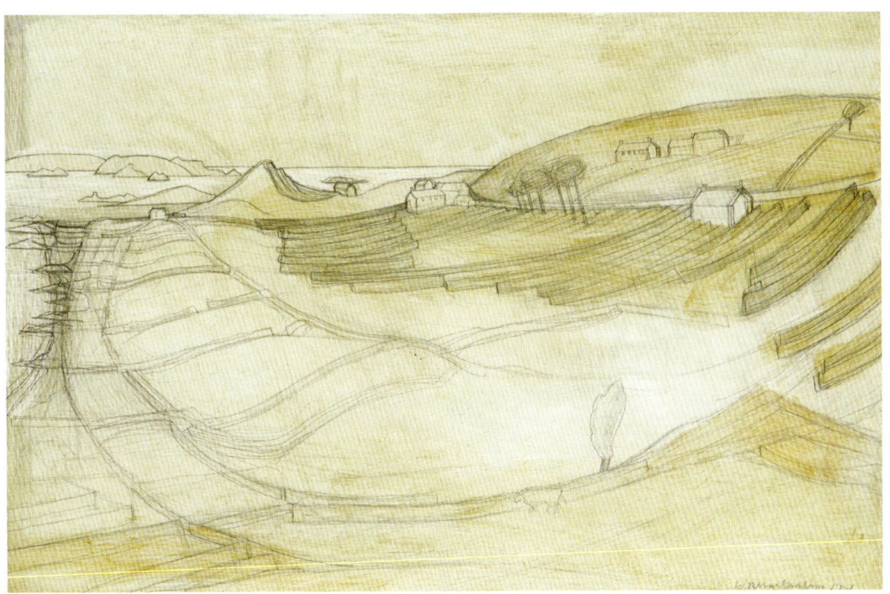

St Martins Lower Town I · 1951 · pen and oil on hardboard · 42.9 x 50.7 cm

clay, Barns-Graham made a number of sizeable drawings around Chiusure that fed into her abstract compositions.

The light and heat of Italy were also conveyed in her drawings by a warm-coloured wash or ground, typically of brown or terracotta, using tempera, oil or gouache thinned with turpentine and rubbed in by hand. She had learnt this technique as a student, though as Nicholson favoured such grounds in the 1950s it is often assumed that she was influenced by him (it may have been the reverse).[15] Using a wash as a base provided texture, depth, tonal variation and atmosphere, and — importantly — it helped Barns-Graham decide where to start, as suggested by her later comment:

> *There is a great excitement and tension before beginning a drawing. The element of shock from the blank paper. The choice of medium, different kinds of pencils on various makes of paper, use of charcoal or chalk, pen and ink or stick dipped in indian ink.*[16]

In the 1960s and 1970s her increasing dependence on geometric shapes and proportional systems lessened her need to seek out new forms in nature, although she continued to draw the landscape in Cornwall and Fife throughout this period. It was only on an extended visit to the island of Orkney in August 1984, when she was in her seventies, that she resumed the practice of responding to a specific location through a sustained body of work. She wrote in her diary:

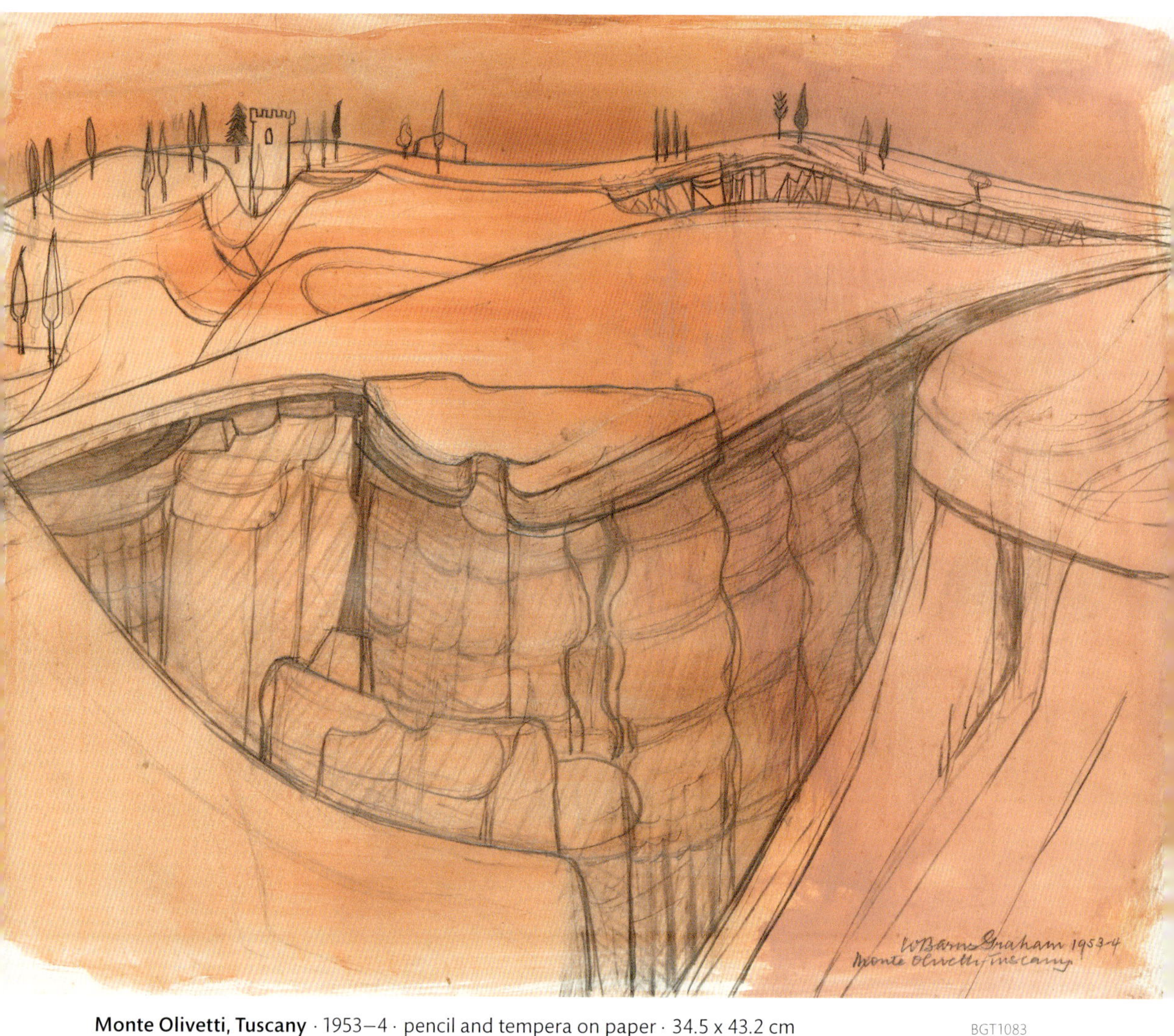

Monte Olivetti, Tuscany · 1953—4 · pencil and tempera on paper · 34.5 x 43.2 cm   BGT1083

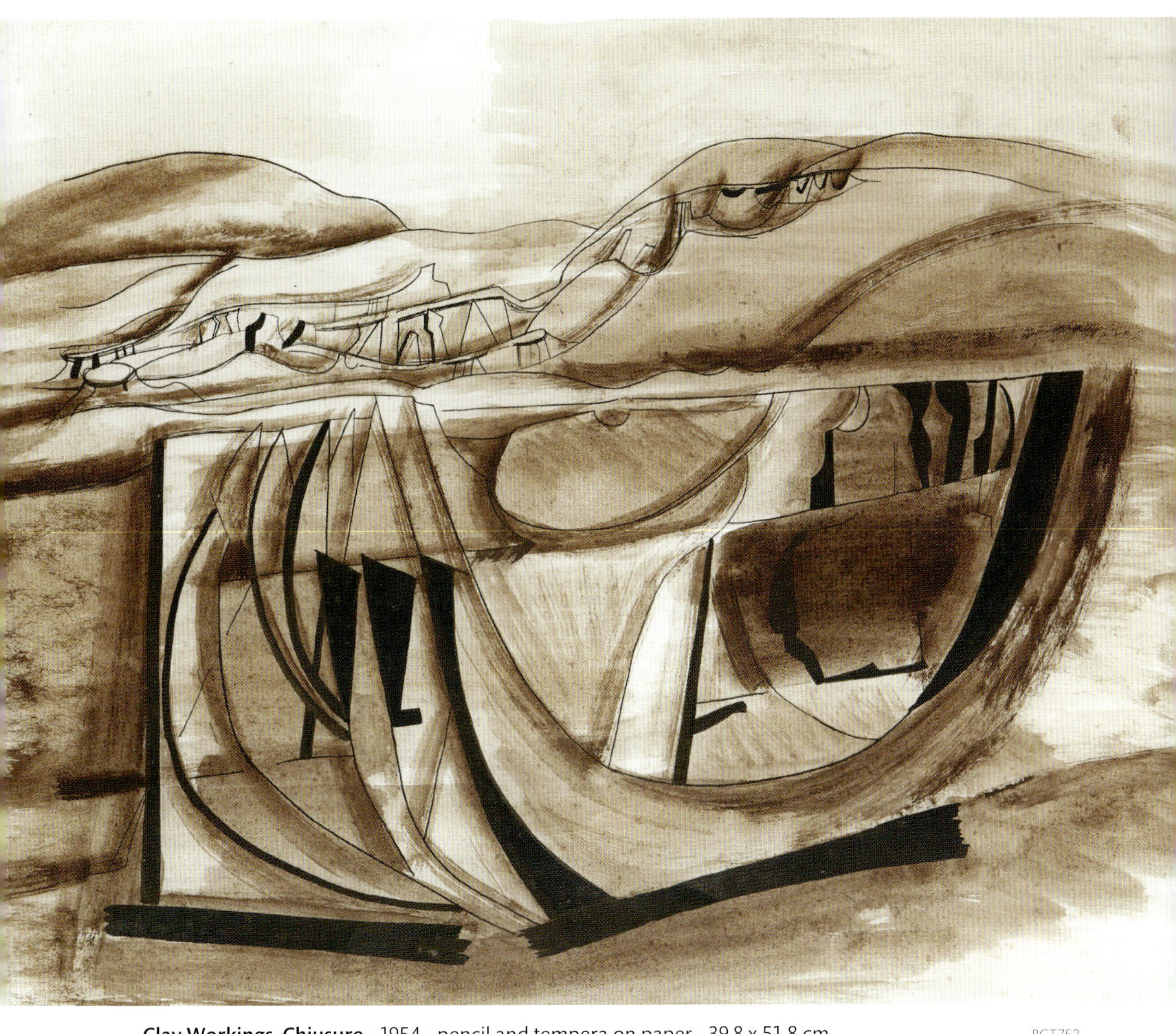

Clay Workings, Chiusure · 1954 · pencil and tempera on paper · 39.8 x 51.8 cm

BGT752

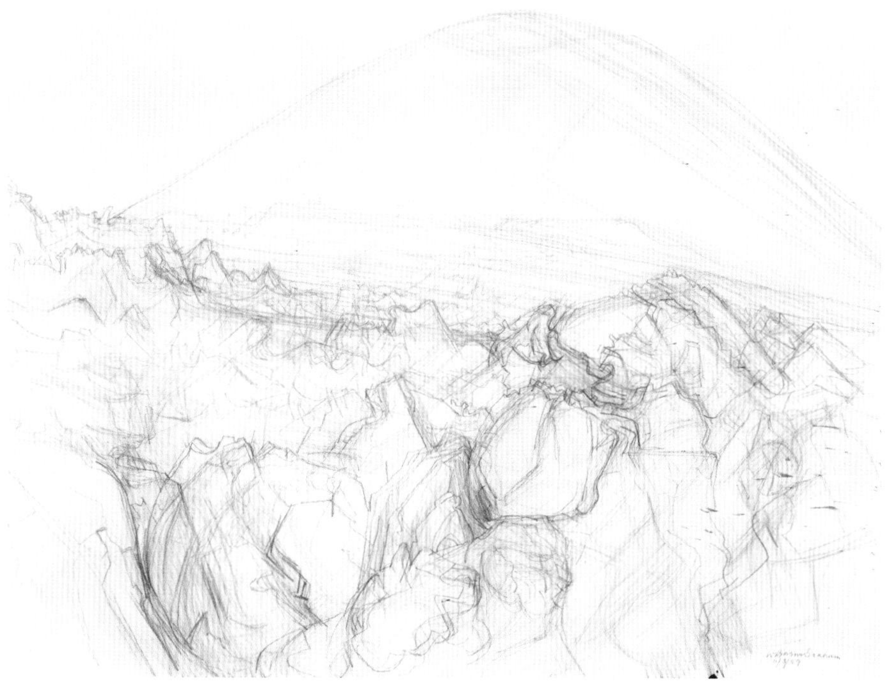

Volcanic Island (Near Montana del Fuego) · 1989 · pencil on paper · 56.5 x 75 cm   BGT669

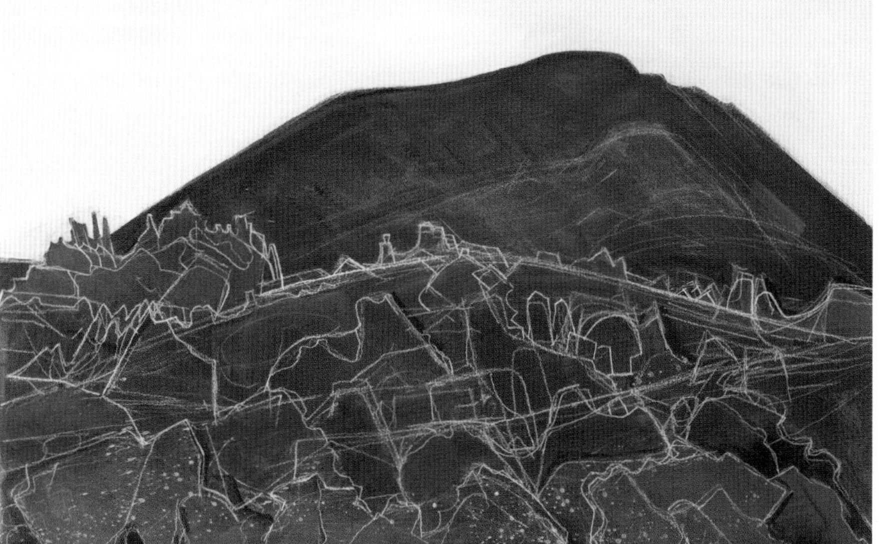

Volcanic Island (Near Montana del Fuego II)   BGT6223
1989 · gouache and chalk on paper · 56.5 x 75 cm

> *So much work ideas are here — drawings colour, shapes, moods, space —
> elongated shapes — & then the light & rock groupings — water movements
> — changes ... it is overwhelming-choked with it all.*[17]

She returned to Orkney in 1985, subsequently making five working trips between
1989 and 1993 to the island of Lanzarote in the Canary Islands, off the coast
of North Africa.

Lanzarote's dry climate suited her constitution and its volcanic landscape
further reconnected her with the central themes of her work. She was instantly
captivated by the drama of the bizarrely crater-pocked terrain and signs of recent
geomorphological activity, such as the smooth, conical mounds of compressed
ash in La Geria, in the centre of the island (left). She made numerous drawings
in front of the motif, her excitement conveyed through experimental mark-
making in a variety of media including white chalk and pastel on a black paper
ground. For example, in *La Geria (Study of Volcanic Rock), Lanzarote* (overleaf),
quivering white lines stutter across the page, evoking the tremors that had once
created the now solidified volcanic crust. On her fourth trip she spent time
drawing the molten lava flows, observing their spiral shapes. She also used
colour in her drawings to capture in her own words, 'the amazing strata bands
of grey, red, darkish brown'.[18] After a 25-year hiatus, sustained absorption in
nature through drawing fuelled a renewed sense of purpose that led to a
remarkable outpouring of creativity in her final decades.

Drawing as meditation

As noted, Barns-Graham used drawing for different purposes. In the early
1960s, in response to the emotional turmoil caused by the failure of her
marriage she sought solace in different religious and philosophical ideas.
The deaths of many friends and colleagues from the 1960s onwards com-
pounded her reflective mood, resulting in a number of contemplative paintings, some as direct tributes others comprising a 'Meditation' series.[19] From the
mid-1970s she made numerous line drawings that suggest the endless flow of
tides, wind currents, substrata, and crystalline patterns (eg. *Glacier Knot*, p. 82)
all of which might also be interpreted as 'meditations', their repetitious marks
suggesting a state of introspective reverie (in the early 1990s she implied this
by titling some of these drawings as meditations). In this respect they owe a
debt to Klee, whose art and ideas, particularly his understanding of natural
processes, were influential in Britain and the United States after his death in

overleaf · **La Geria (Study of Volcanic Rock), Lanzarote**
1990 · chalk and pastel on black paper · 53.4 x 70.2 cm · Martin Kemp Collection

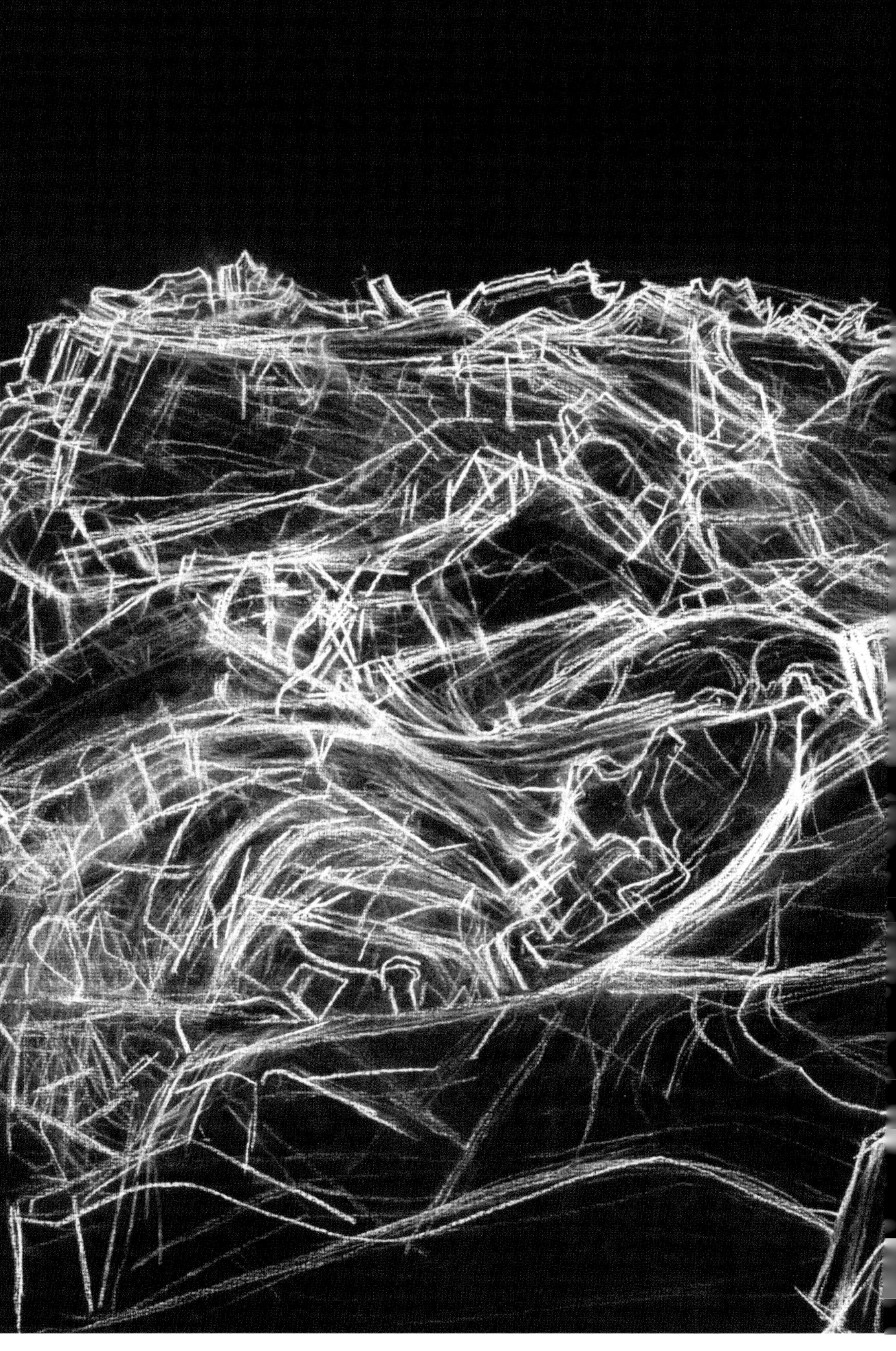

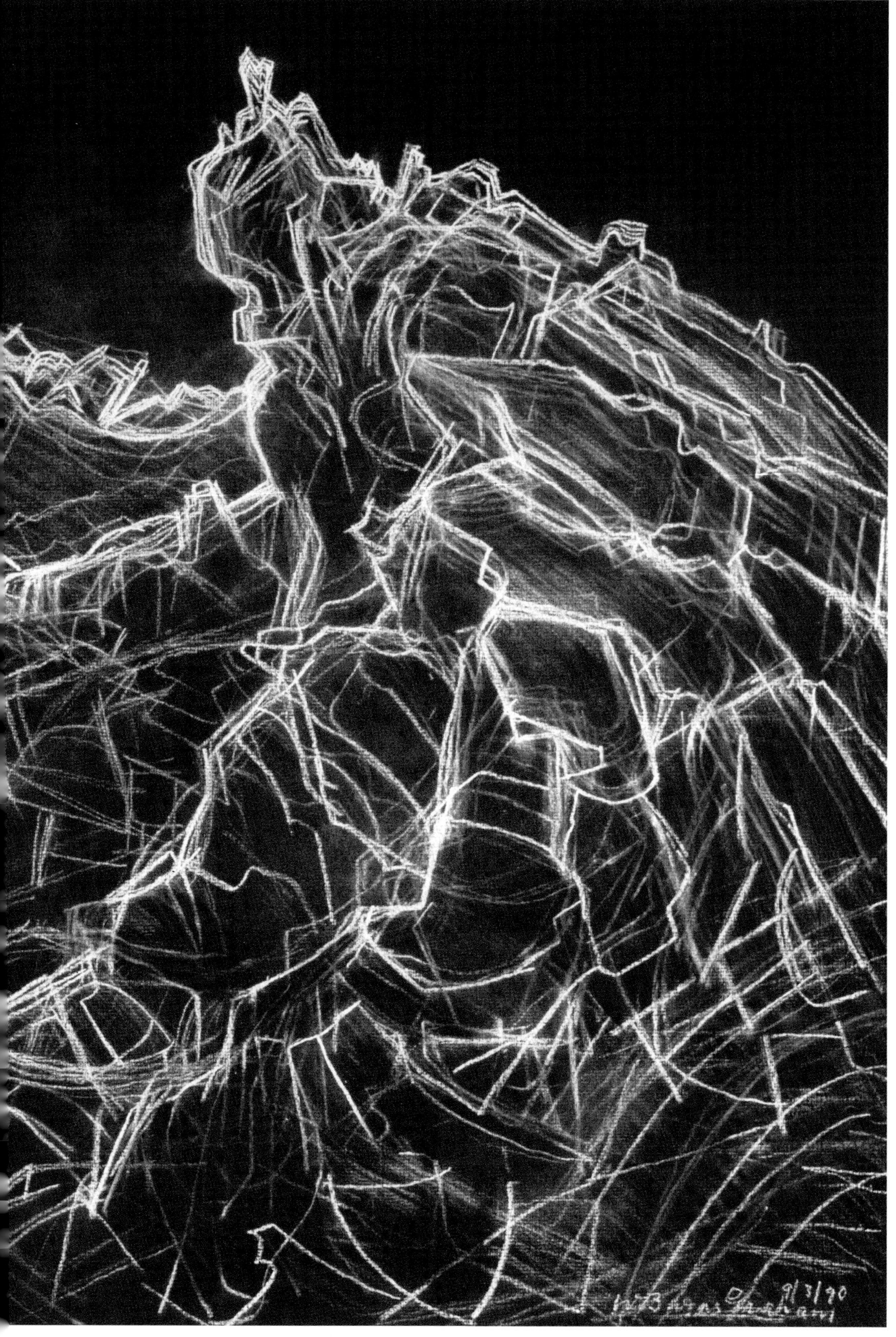

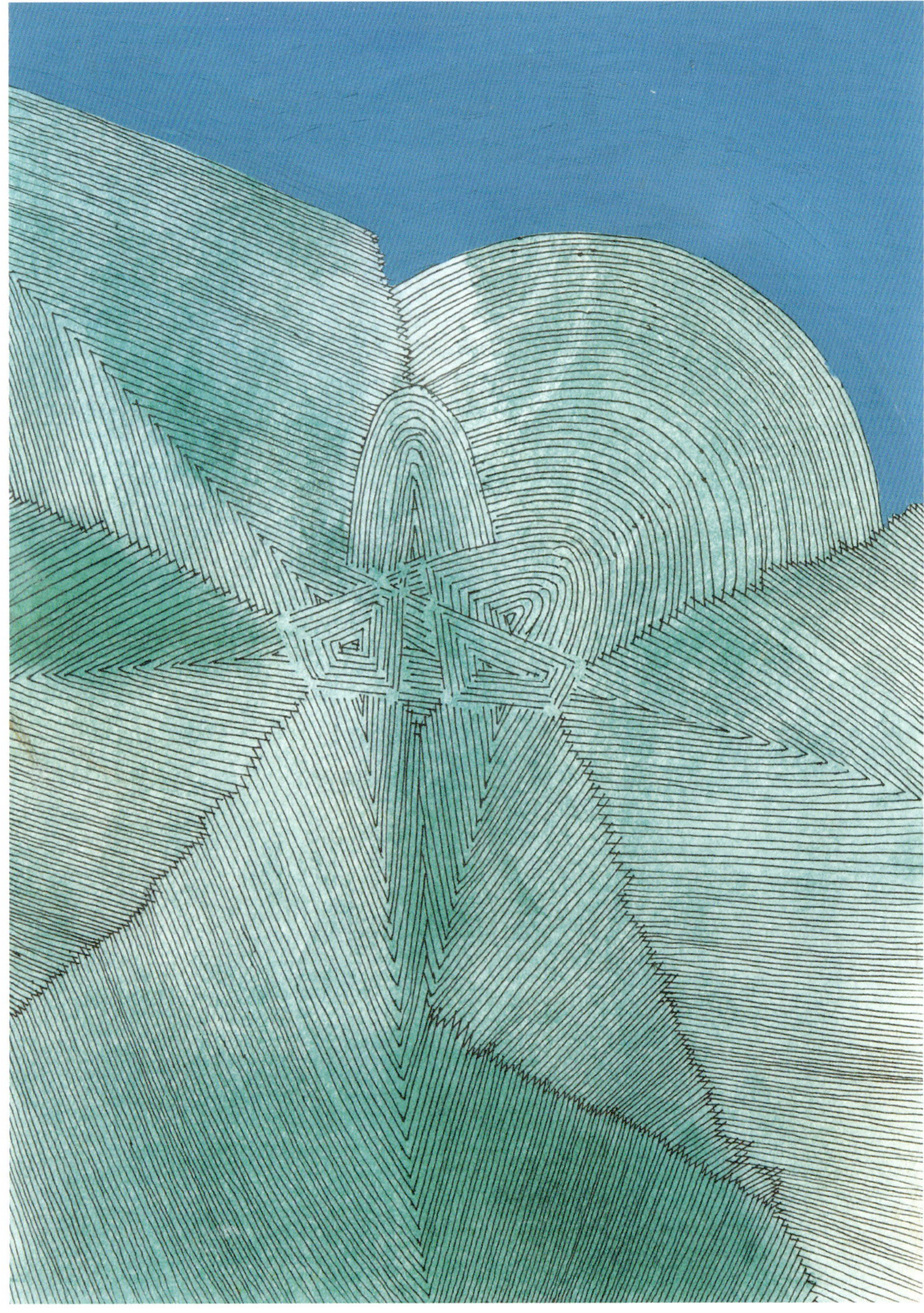

Glacier Knot · 1979 · pen, ink and mixed media on board · 27.2 x 20 cm

1940. His writings were published as the *Pedagogical Sketchbook* in the 1920s (English translation 1953) and *The Thinking Eye* (1956, English translation 1961). Barns-Graham referred in particular to Klee's notion of taking a line for a walk when explaining her method of summoning up nature's cadences from memory through drawing:

> *For a session of drawing I may exclusively use linear ideas: an abstraction of what has been observed, first drawing a grid or a mathematical plan using a series of long and short lines over or against this grid, building up a rhythm to allow the unexpected as curves or wave lines encouraging imagination and becoming creative. These rhythms suggest flowing forms, water, grass and wind movements, or lines for the pleasure of themselves. Paul Klee suggests, 'We take a walk with a line.'*[20]

In the lines of her small, intricate drawings or doodles of waves, wind and sand, she allowed her store of unconscious perceptions of the world free rein. Her meditative use of line — the primary element of drawing — can also be seen in the calligraphic marks of her paintings of the late 1950s, which in part show her responding to the influences of the Far East in modern art, as seen in the paintings of Soulages, Bernard Leach's friend Mark Tobey (1890–1976) and Robert Motherwell, whose work she admired. The calligraphic, linear brushstroke motifs that dominated her work from the mid-1990s onwards were similarly executed as a form of drawing in paint.

Whether used to translate her perceptions in front of nature, fusing her 'inner seeing' and 'outer sensing' to create a language of abstraction, or as a way of accessing memories and feelings, drawing remained fundamental to Barns-Graham's creative process, culminating in the fusion of line and colour in her late works. Alongside a number of staged studio photographs, more informal photographs captured the artist drawing in all weather conditions on her customary half imperial size paper, rapt in concentration or striding through the landscape seeking out her subject. Perhaps to understand the artist, we need look no further than her drawings: 'My drawings are not pretentious, needing constantly to search and abstract, to communicate; our work is what we are.'[21]

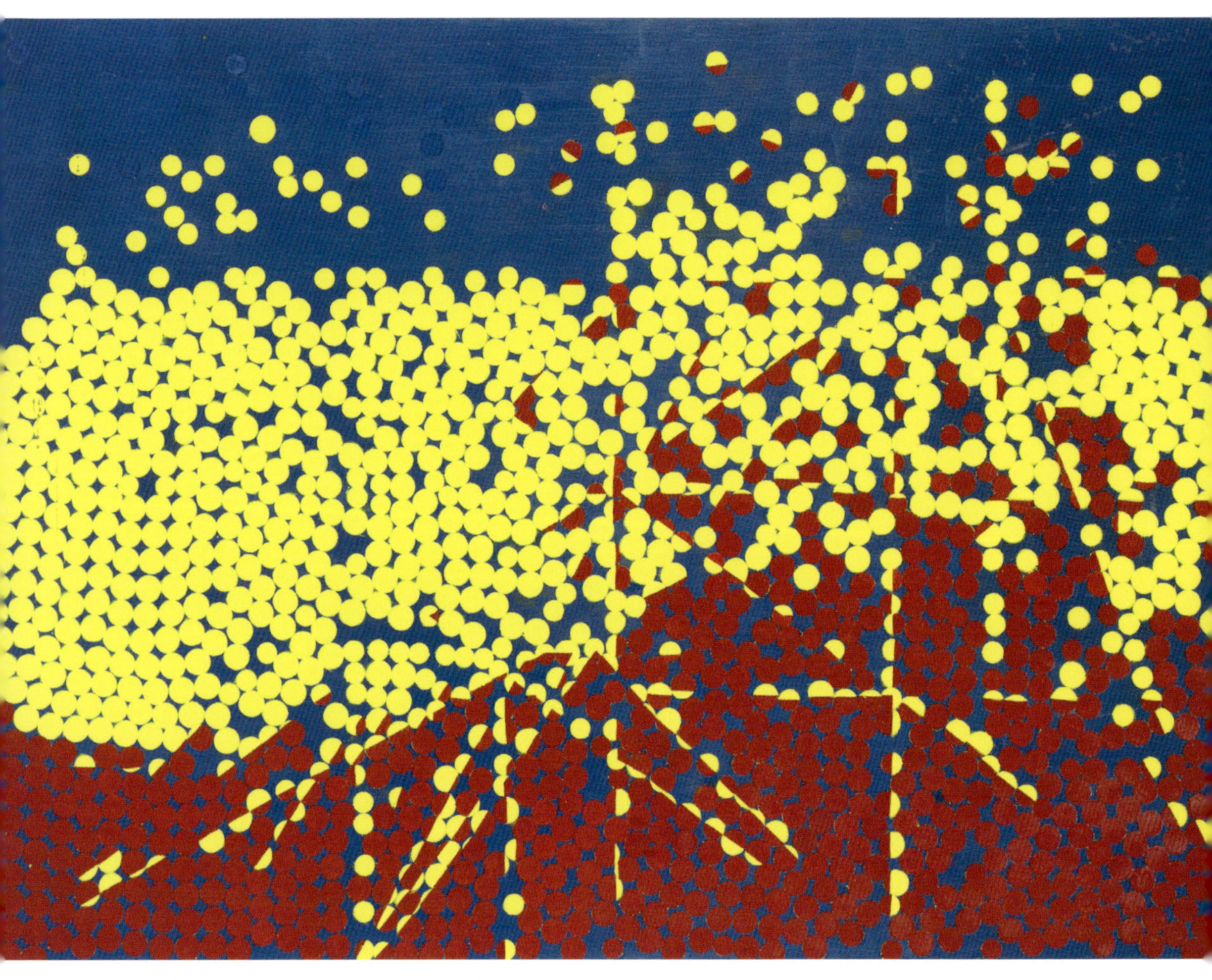

Zoom · 1971 · oil and acrylic on hardboard · 58.5 x 81.2 cm

BGT377

84

5 Colour 'looking in – looking out'[1]

It became clear to me that new frameworks of pure colour must be created, based on what colour demanded and also that colour, in its turn, must pass out of the pictorial mix into an independent unity, a structure in which it would be at once individual in a collective environment and individually independent.

Kasimir Malevich (1878–1935)[2]

In 2002 Barns-Graham made a note on writings by the Russian Suprematist painter Kasimir Malevich indicating her enthusiasm for his idea that colour is the essence of painting, and that each form is individual and free, constituting a world in itself.[3] While contrasts of mood, compositional structure and gesture in her work all intensified as she neared the end of her life, above all else her late work was governed by the uninhibited manipulation of saturated colour.

This final chapter considers the role of colour in Barns-Graham's work, with particular reference to works made in her last decades, when a new sense of freedom and sheer joy imbued her output. Her palette varied throughout her career, responding to specific places and prevailing interests in colour theories, both of which seemed to interest her in equal measure. However, in the late works colour appears more than ever to have taken on a highly personal meaning. During this extraordinarily creative phase, the fundamental elements of picture making – form, space, texture and line – practiced almost daily over many years, were expertly deployed in a prolific period of production. Aware that her life was drawing to a close, she told a critic in 2001: 'Now I am at the stage of urgency. My theme is celebration of life, joy, the importance of colour, form, space and texture.'[4]

Geometry and underlying grids remained important principles but her painting became more fluid and intuitive, and she allowed chance to play a greater role in her creative process. Proportional structures provided frameworks for the display of undiluted colour, as she wrote in a statement published in 2000: 'Colour as colour, texture as texture, so blue is not sky, green is not grass, but is an object in itself, so that it is itself.'[5]

While revisiting the directional lines and rhythms of earlier abstract compositions, the late works represent a letting go — or as she put it 'letting rip' — and perhaps a final yielding to and delighting in her secret, synesthetic world of colour associations.[6] Barns-Graham may have hinted at these private meanings in an interview of 1994, declaring that she didn't want her paintings to be representational, preferring them: '… to be an enjoyment of colour, vibration and shape. And they're not as innocent as they look.'[7] Through an orchestration of pure colour Barns-Graham believed she had found her own voice.[8]

Synaesthesia is a neurological condition that connects normally distinct senses, so for example, a synesthetic might taste sound or hear colour. The effects of synaesthesia are involuntary, consistent and memorable, and usually develop in childhood, though it can take time for a synesthetic to recognise their unique perceptions. Barns-Graham experienced a form of synaesthesia that associates colour with people, places, numbers and letters, with a particular emphasis on word and colour association, known as grapheme-colour synaesthesia.[9] Robert Adam observed Barns-Graham's astonishing ability to distinguish between Cadmium Yellow No. 8 and No. 9, and recalled her synaesthesia:

This meant that sensations she experienced were translated intuitively into specific colours with attendant harmonies and discords. I remember going through the alphabet with her once, and her telling me without hesitation the particular colour she associated with each letter.[10]

The subtlety of each colour association — its depth and variety — held a personal emotional value for her and this unusual 'gift' undoubtedly contributed to Barns-Graham's view that her life as an artist was a vocation rather than a career.

She also recognised colour as part of her cultural inheritance. The notion that the Scottish artist's particular responsiveness to colour was innate, shaped by the Scottish landscape and northern climate, had been promulgated as a national characteristic since at least the early twentieth century. While such essentialist evaluations of national tendencies are no longer tenable, as a student in Edinburgh Barns-Graham would have known that colour was a defining characteristic of Scottish modernism, exemplified by the 'Scottish Colourists'. These artists had absorbed the lessons of French modernism, from Édouard Manet (1832–1883) and Cézanne to the expressive use of colour exemplified by Vincent Van Gogh (1853–1890) and the Fauves.

Barns-Graham held leading 'Scottish Colourist' S.J. Peploe in high regard, and was taught by the charismatic William Gillies whose love of colour was informed by the works of André Derain (1880–1954), Henri Matisse (1869–1954) and Bonnard.[11] By the 1950s the term 'Scottish Colourists' was widely used, but only later in the 1980s associated exclusively with Peploe, J.D. Fergusson (1874–1961), G.L. Hunter (1877–1931) and F.C.B. Cadell (1883–1937), on account of their fondness for vivid colour and fluid brushwork.[12] Barns-Graham reconnected with this aspect of her cultural heritage later in life, in the context of a wider re-evaluation of national traditions in art and the increased visibility of the 'Scottish Colourists' in the 1980s.

Like those of other artists, Barns-Graham's colour preferences shifted in relation to her aims and in response to changing trends or currents in art practice. Through colour she signalled her aesthetic and philosophical interests and allegiances. For example, in the 1940s the 'St Ives' painters were influenced by Alfred Wallis, particularly after his death in 1942. In 1980, when asked how he had affected her work, Barns-Graham referred to his colours rather than any other aspect of his painting: 'Yes, I think Alfred Wallis's greys and greens spoke to me, and did have a big impact on me because they were true.'[13] She briefly knew Wallis, who became something of a talisman for 'St Ives' thanks largely to the promotion of his work by Nicholson and Stokes, and owned three of his paintings, gifted to her by Nicholson, Sven Berlin and Mary Buchanan. But she also sought to express her own identity through colour. In *Studio Interior (Red Stool)* of 1945, a yellow jug perched on a red stool, stands out against a neutral interior. Her choice of primary colours points to pre-war international modernism but also to the characteristic primary hues favoured by the 'Scottish Colourists', seen for example in Peploe's *Interior with Japanese Print* (c.1916) or Cadell's *Interior, The Red Chair* (c.1928).

'St Ives' abstraction became recognised for its responsiveness to place, especially to the colour and light of Cornwall's rocky, sea-fringed peninsula. Throughout her career, Barns-Graham's palette was influenced by her experience of specific natural environments and phenomena, in Cornwall and elsewhere, but her colour choices were sophisticated statements rather than reportage.

'St Ives' artists for a time at least responded to Cornwall through the lens of Alfred Wallis's colour and tonal range, but art history offered alternative filters.

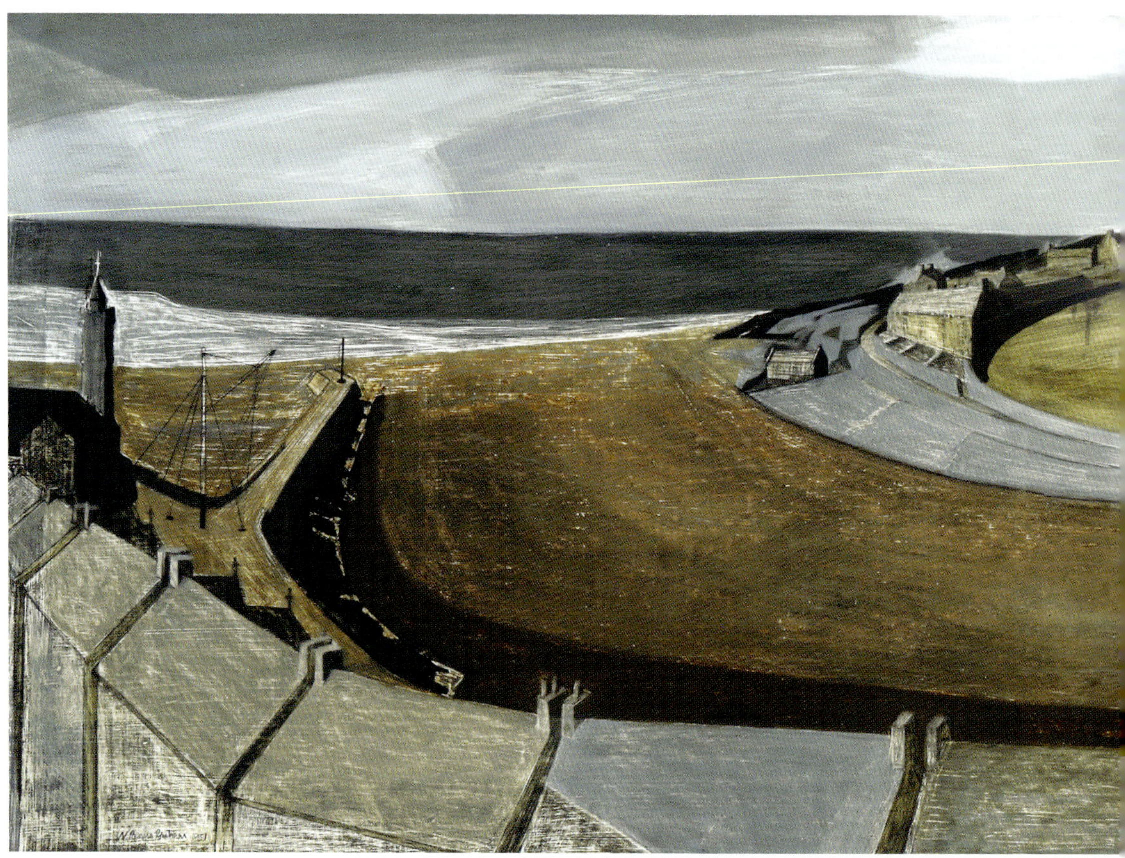

Cornish Landscape (Evening), Porthleven · 1951 · oil on canvas · 61 x 167 cm

For example, in *Cornish Landscape (Evening), Porthleven* of 1951 (above), Barns-Graham bathed the harbour scene in colour inspired by the fifteenth-century Italian painter Piero della Francesca (1416—1492), referring to the painting in a letter to her parents as: '... like an early Italian painting in colour. Browns and blue greys'.[14] She consistently used colour lyrically to evoke rather than describe. This is highlighted by works resulting from her visit to Spain and the Balearic Islands in 1958, which are infused with colours and tones such as earthy russet and ochre, red, orange and sharp citrus that are associated with Spanish culture as much as its climate and landscape (eg. *Lime and Flame*, p. 90).

Colour researches

From the early 1960s Barns-Graham turned her attention to sustained research into the interaction of shape and colour in the series 'Order and Disorder of Things of a Kind' (1964-72), expressing her intentions in an article published in February 1962:

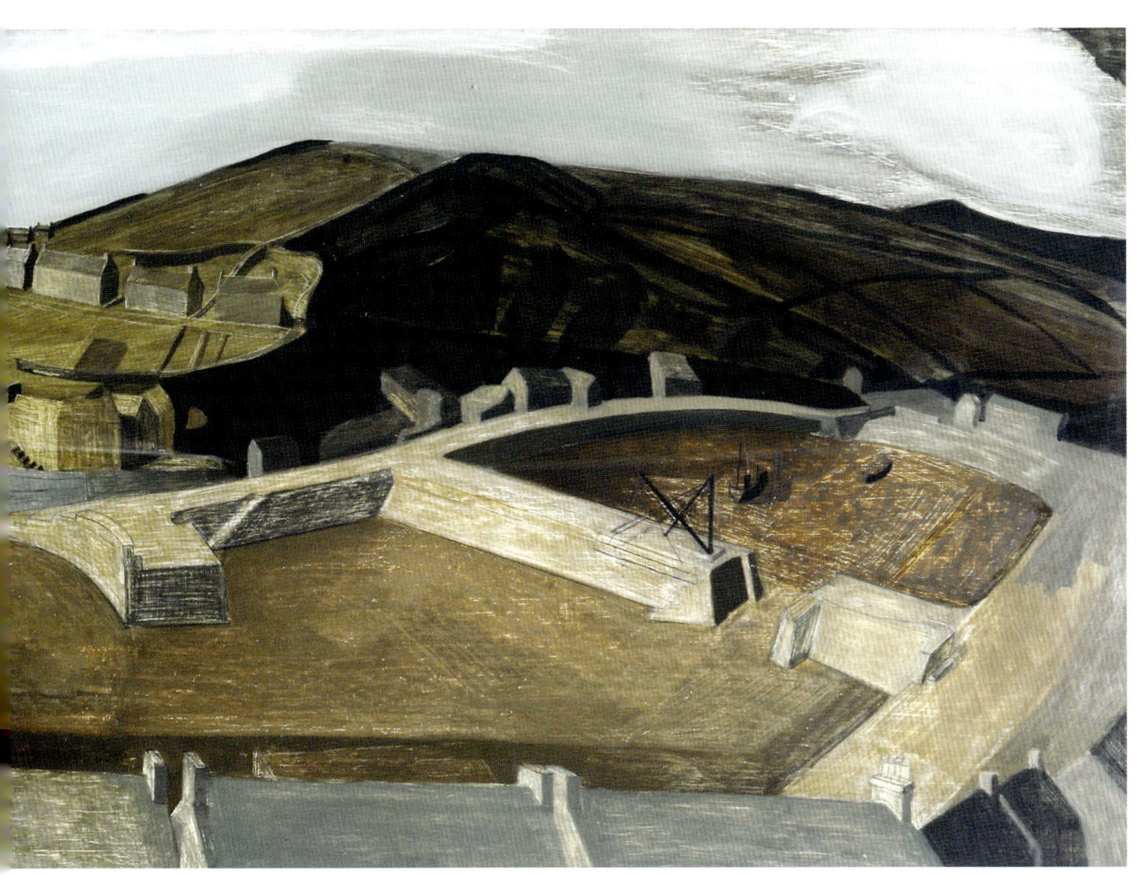

I want my work to be a simple statement. To have an atmosphere and integrity ... To have interesting space relationships, relationships of colour, and colour to form — that is form suggesting colour and vice versa.[15]

As an inquiry into the properties of formal elements, especially colour, this major body of work was informed by the pedagogic methods of the new Basic Design course at Leeds College of Art, introduced while Barns-Graham was teaching there during the academic year 1956–1957. Founded on Bauhaus principles, the course aimed through experimental exercises to encourage visual literacy in the use of colour, alongside understanding of form and the construction of space.

Limiting shapes to square and circle motifs, this series is striking in its range and use of colour. Monochrome paintings allowed Barns-Graham to focus on the interaction and articulation of shapes on the canvas, but the juxtaposition of calculated proportions of unmodulated colours, particularly complementary colours such as red and green, amplified the sensation of movement or

tensions within the picture, as seen in *Two Reds and Two Greens* (right).
In her colour choices — some of which appear discordant or jarring — and
colour gradations, and by varying the relationship of shape to background,
Barns-Graham explored colour as a material, testing its behaviours in different
combinations and circumstances. Her colour experiments continued into the
later 1970s, for instance in an ambitious group of paintings that investigate
colour value through precise gradations, as seen for example in *Warm Up,
Cool Down* (p. 92).

The principle of complementary colours or 'simultaneous contrast' had been
established in the nineteenth century by the French chemist Michel Eugène
Chevreul (1786–1889), whose theories were absorbed by the post-Impressionist
pointillistes and in the teaching of colour theory at the Bauhaus in Germany in
the 1920s. Josef Albers (1888–1976), who left the Bauhaus in 1930 for the USA,
was particularly interested in the idea of colour as active and subjective. Basing
his influential colour course on Chevreul's discoveries and involving students
in multiple colour experiments, Albers demonstrated that colours in themselves
are not absolute and stable, but constantly changing in relation to their context.[16]
Like Wassily Kandinsky (1866–1944), a former colleague at the Bauhaus, Albers
developed a metaphorical language, in which colours were described as musical
notes, flavours, and places, an alternative vocabulary of colour that resonated

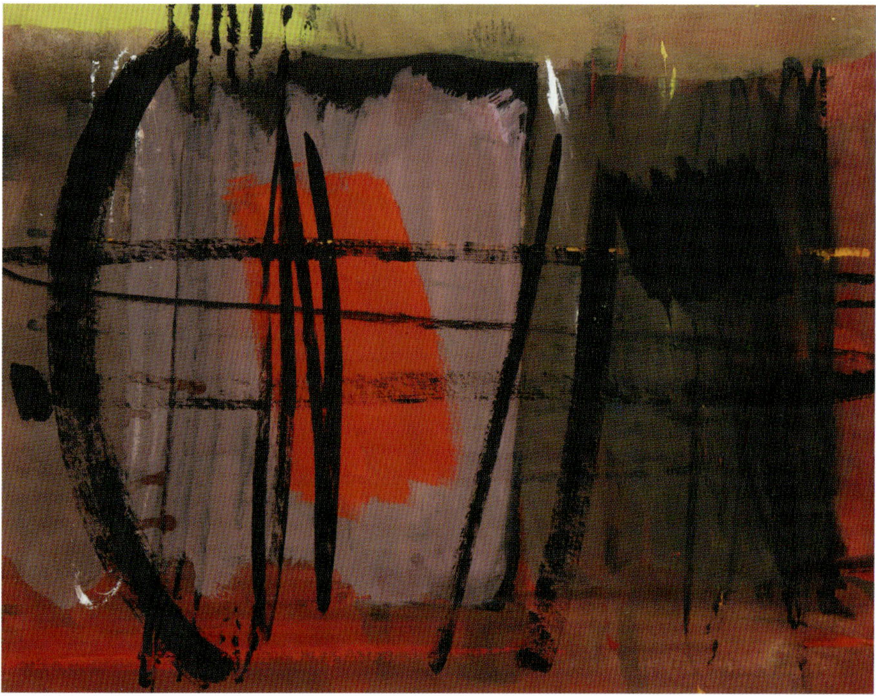

Lime and Flame · 1958 · gouache on paper · 40.8 x 51.5 cm   BGT584

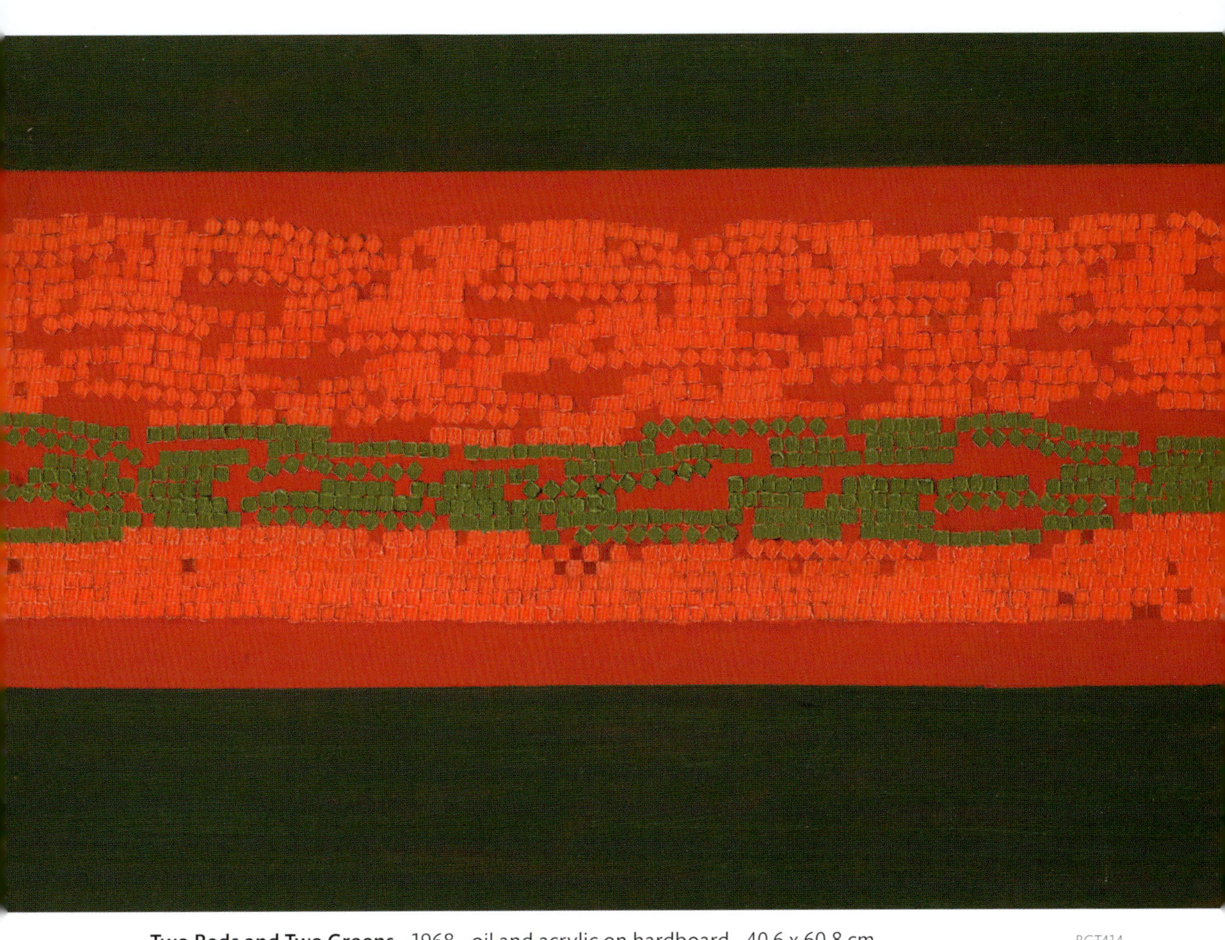

Two Reds and Two Greens · 1968 · oil and acrylic on hardboard · 40.6 x 60.8 cm   BGT414

overleaf · **Warm Up, Cool Down** · 1979 · acrylic on canvas, 92.3 x 123 cm · BGT383

with Barns-Graham's synesthetic perceptions. For Albers, colours were timid or aggressive protagonists, capable of forming dictatorships or democracies.[17] Barns-Graham's own understanding of the ability of colour to take on attitudes, to express character traits, was finely tuned by her exhaustive experimentation in the studio, and would be fully exploited in her mature paintings.

Importantly, though working with preconceived structures she continued to apply colour expressively to convey mood, atmospherics and transcendental themes. For example, an 'Order and Disorder' painting such as *Assembly of Nine* (right) refers to the Baha'i faith in which nine members are required for a meeting, its square forms animated by flicks of red, and its radiating yellow centre symbolises spirituality.[18]

'Letting rip'

Even Barns-Graham's most rigorously abstract work retained personal or emotional content through her use of colour. Pages from notebooks in the artist's archive reveal that she used her synesthetic association of letters and colours as a protocol for determining abstract paintings that would have her own personal meaning. As she grew older, she began to realise that her sensitivity to colour was unique. Aged 76 she visited the Tate Gallery's 'Late Picasso' exhibition and was struck by the daring, prolific output of an artist in old age, summed up by Michel Leiris's introduction to the exhibition catalogue:

> *And working thus, at double tempo, does Picasso … not seem to have let off a wonderful last set-piece, in a spectacular affirmation, thanks to the boldness of a line freed from all stylistic constraints and to the intensity of his colours, that although death was drawing near, he was more alive than ever?*[19]

It is telling that in the back of her copy of the catalogue she diligently noted the discrepancies between the reproduced colour plates and what she had seen in the gallery. It was the trueness of Picasso's colour that she wanted to remember. And, without holding back, it was through colour she pursued her own glorious final act.

With a renewed interest in the work of Antoni Tàpies (1923—2012), Miró, and also Picasso, she reprised the gestural style of her earlier Spanish paintings; only now her brush mark was used to highlight the subject of her work: colour. Her profound grasp of the properties and behaviours of colour as pigment and material coalesced with her sensitivity to colour as she perceived it in nature. Trips to Orkney, Lanzarote and Barcelona between the mid-1980s and early 1990s prompted new abstract paintings infused with rich colour, while forms

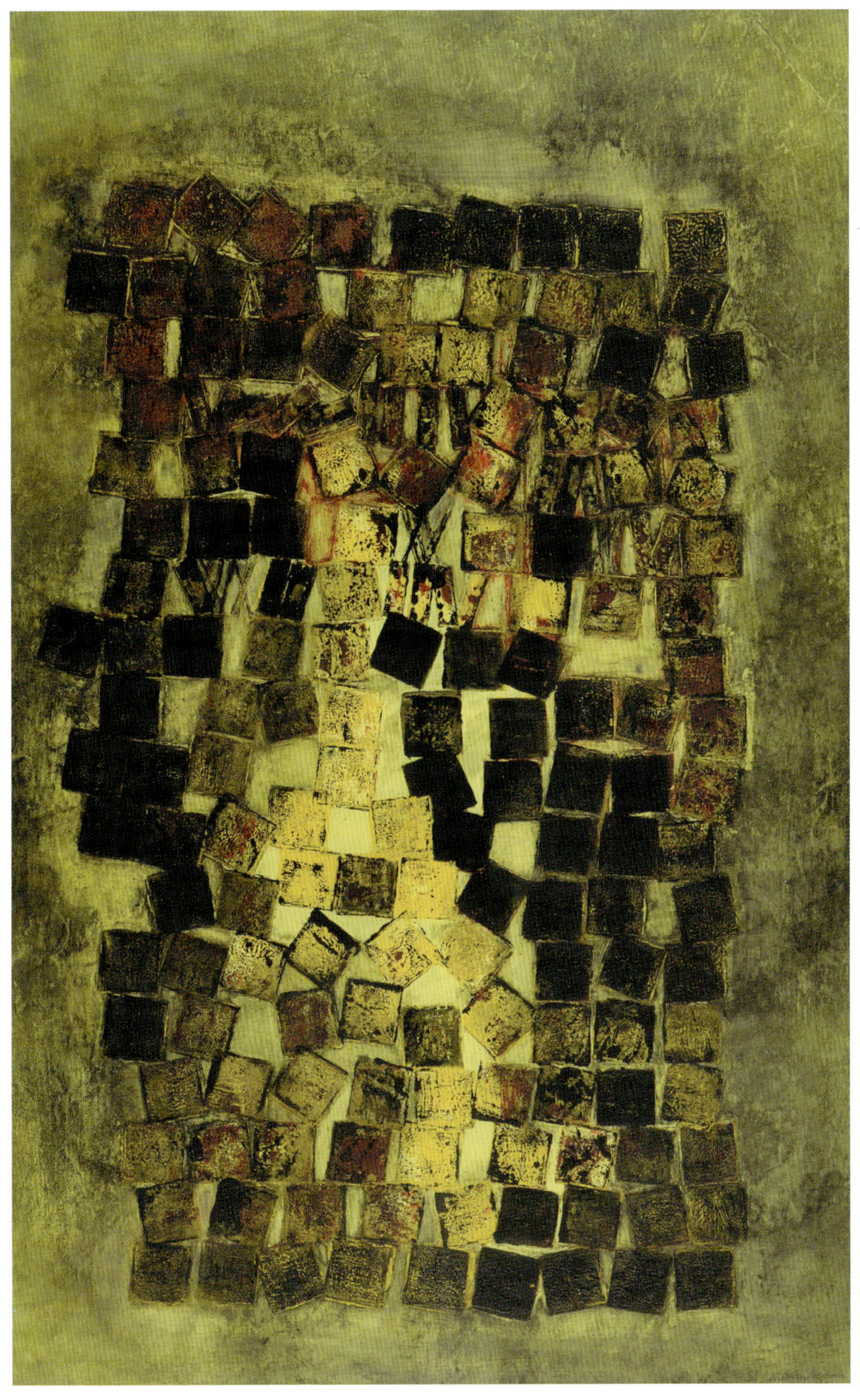

Assembly of Nine · 1964 · oil on hardboard · 90.5 x 57.4 cm

BGT558

and shapes stored in her memory resurfaced in paintings of highly-coloured mushrooms found in Balmungo's garden.[20]

The liberation of colour in her work was fully realised in her extensive 'Scorpio' series of the mid-to-late-1990s (right). In these paintings, friezes of vertical or diagonal brushstrokes in a variety of colours — cadmium red, ultramarine and cerulean blue, yellow, purple, green and orange — dance across a landscape ground. Each coloured band is unique. Varying subtly in texture, width and length, some loaded with paint seem to shout, while other more transparent strokes seem to whisper. Compositionally, the spatial dynamism of these coloured bands — and the artist's attention to proportional balance — refer back to works such as *Red Painting* (p. 36), and *Expanding White Panels* (below). However, as distinct elements with individual characteristics her brushstrokes are held in rhythmic conversations, and in this regard they clearly relate to her 'Things of a kind' theme. Working across a group of half a dozen paintings simultaneously on paper in fast-drying acrylic enabled the artist to create a group of interrelated images. Lynne Green has described the artist's working method, which resembles jazz improvisation:

> *Taking a single colour and the dominant gesture of a single brushstroke, she sets down her mark on each sheet in turn, then takes up another colour and so on, as the images evolve.*[21]

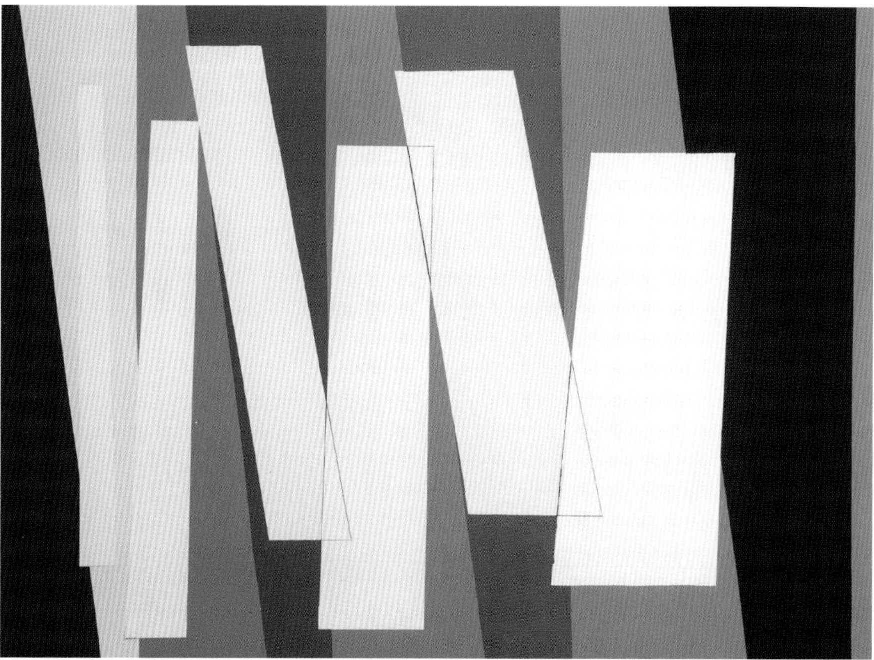

Expanding White Panels · 1980 · oil on hardboard · 85.5 x 105.5 cm   BGT379

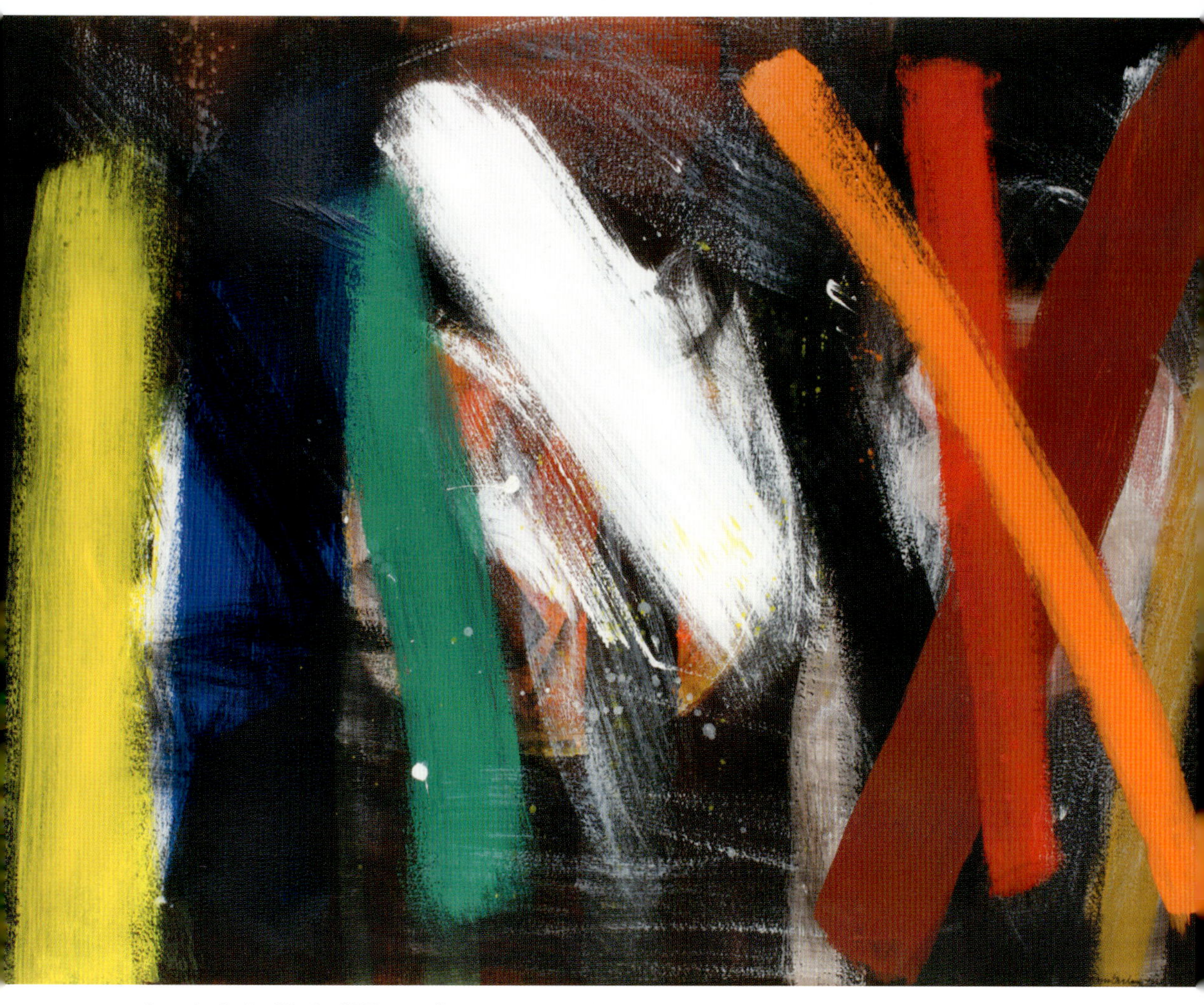

Scorpio Series No. 1 · 1995 · acrylic on paper · 55.6 x 75.5 cm

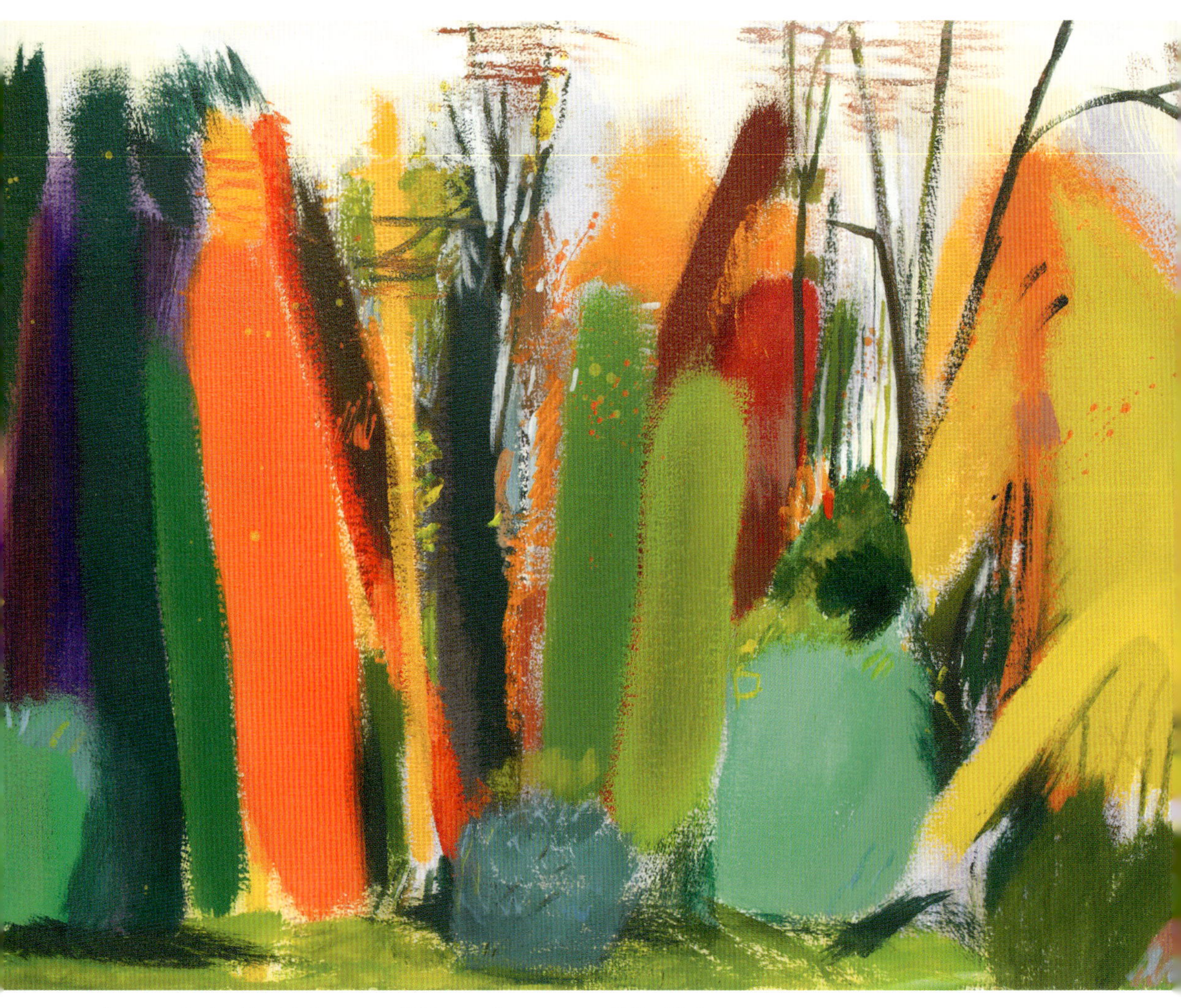

Autumn Series No. 4 Balmungo · 1998 · acrylic on paper · 57.9 x 75.6 cm   BGT3019

For Barns-Graham these colour brushstrokes were ostensibly independent abstract forms, like musical notes, diverse in pitch and tone. Similar vertical bands of colour also appear as tree trunks and foliage in paintings such as *Autumn Series No. 4 Balmungo* (left), suggesting both the idea of visual sounds or notes in nature and the deep interconnection and indivisibility of her inner vision and outer perceptions.

The layering of coloured elements established in the 'Scorpio' series informed Barns-Graham's innovative silkscreen prints made in collaboration with Carol Robertson and Robert Adam of the Graal Press from 1998 to her death. Facilitated by Robertson, who approached silkscreen printing as 'painting in slow motion', and using Graal's innovative water-based pigments, the process allowed Barns-Graham to work with greater spontaneity and precision in terms of colour relationships, tonal range and intensity.[22] Remarkably, some prints comprise fifteen layers of colour.[23] Silkscreen printing also encouraged her to generate compositions using chance. Single marks painted on to separate sheets of film would be thrown into the air, falling to the floor in unexpected patterns.[24] She later used film positives in her painting process, a technique that made it possible to work without becoming too exhausted.

Colour also features in other late paintings that address Barns-Graham's pre-occupation with nature's elusive, powerful elemental forces, and the magnitude and mystery of the constellations. The ambitious *Jupiter's Dream* (1998), for example, offers a prismatic, kaleidoscopic vision of space, while reverberating colour contrasts in works such as *Volcanic Wind* (p. 102) evoke the extreme and violent sensations of heat and speed. Her use of black and white also became more expressive; a pitch black band often asserts itself or lurks in the back-ground, and in the lyrical 'Gaia' series dematerialising spheres of black paint are suspended in space, like dark matter, present yet void.

In Barns-Graham's late works, line and colour merge to emphasise the power of her brushwork — a direct cipher for the sweep of her arm, or the flick of her wrist — as a form of drawing in pure pigment. In her 'Easter' series of 2001 (overleaf), the artist radically reduced the compositional elements to one or two vertical brushstrokes and a circle, using a limited palette of blue, black, grey and white. These bold, textured brushstrokes draw attention to the weight and pressure of the artist's hand and the time taken to execute the mark from start to finish.

In her last decades, the blurring of inner feelings, memory and external per-ception of the world intensified. For example, the circle, a universal symbol of the infinite, reappeared as a recurring motif, representing for the artist 'a wonderful spiritual movement — the highest form'.[25] But it also conjured up the circular studio window of her childhood home, or the sun and the moon rising and setting over Porthmeor beach. Similarly, Barns-Graham's preference for the colour blue as a ground in many of her later paintings and prints was influenced by Cornwall's azure sea and expansive sky. Such immersive blue fields also invoke a spiritual mood; the Latin root for ultramarine is beyond (ultra) and sea (mare), while a colour such as cerulean blue, in French *bleu céleste* or heavenly

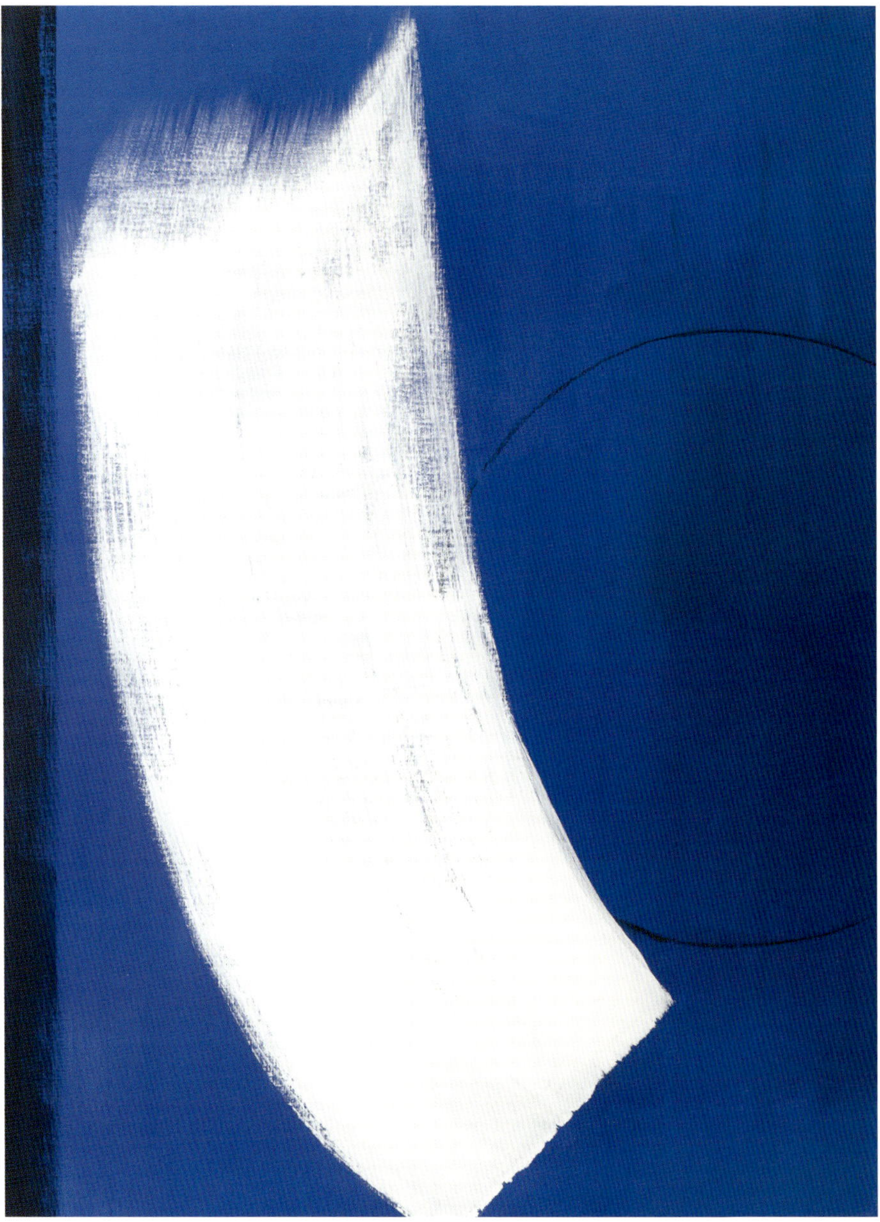

Vertical Movement (Easter Series) Blue · 2001 · acrylic on paper · 121.6 x 91.2 cm   BGT1319

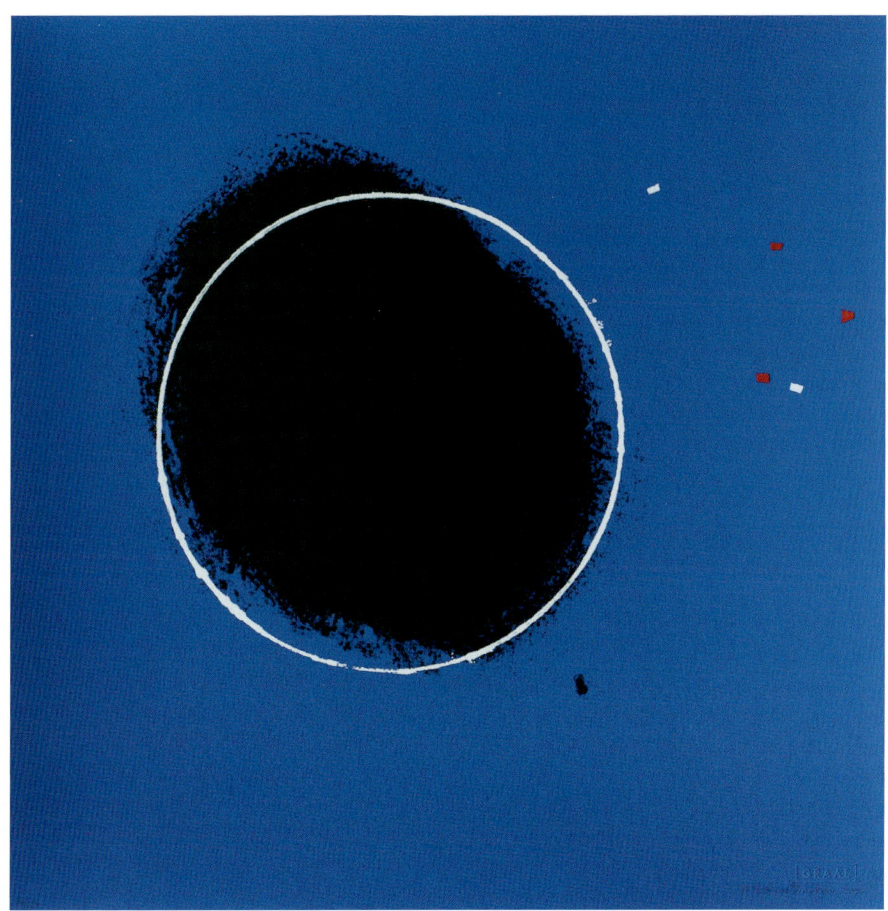

White Circle Series I · 2003 · screenprint on paper · 56 x 56 cm   edition of 70

blue, expresses a sense of the divine, of spiritual consciousness or feeling. But Barns-Graham's blue grounds also possibly refer to perception itself, emphasising human interconnectedness with nature's processes and phenomena. Interestingly, our optical response to blue light, enhanced by means of a special receptor, plays a key role in establishing the circadian rhythm that structures patterns of waking and sleeping, aligning us with nature's ancient cycle.[26]

Barns-Graham identified with the idea of the 'looking in-looking out' kind of artist, as described by her artist friend Winifred Nicholson (1893–1981), for whom emotion and memory transform the experience of nature through art-making.[27] In this sense she remained essentially a 'St Ives' artist, but one or whom colour, memory and meaning were indivisible.

overleaf · **Volcanic Wind** · 1994 · oil on canvas · 122 x 167.5 cm · BGT6454

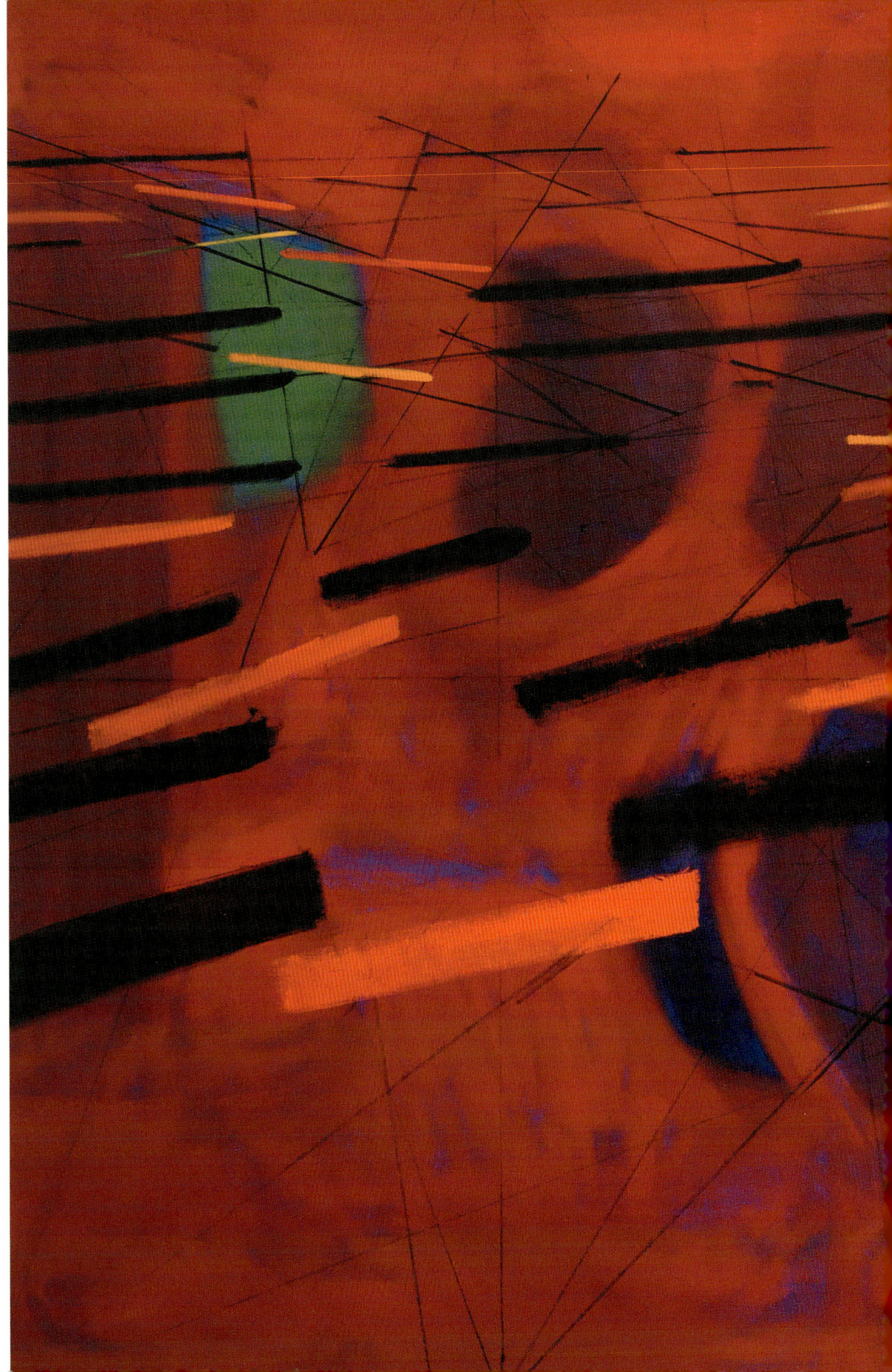

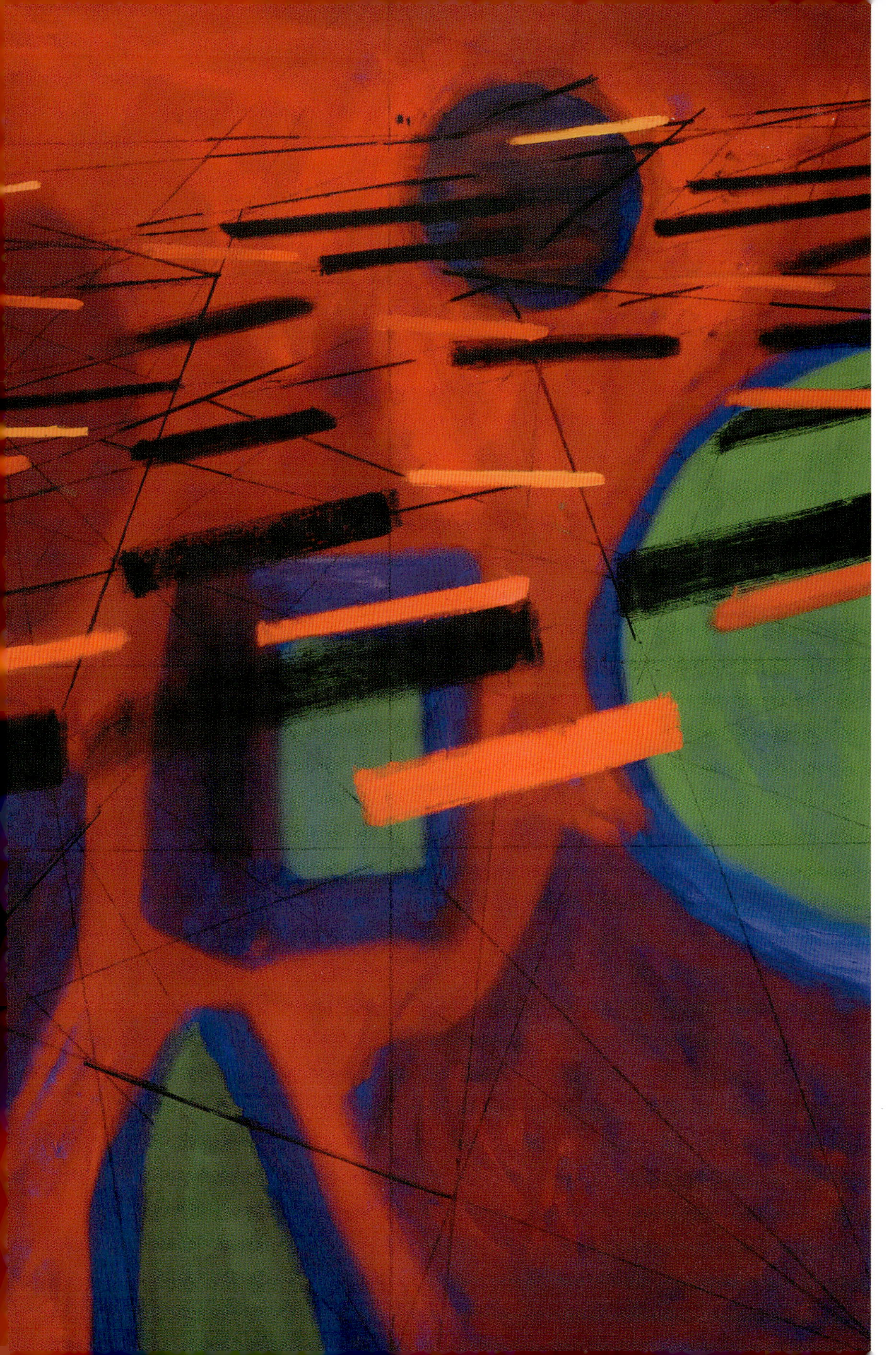

Notes

Introduction

1. Lynne Green, *Wilhelmina Barns-Graham: A Studio Life* (London: Lund Humphries, 2001, revised 2011), p. 27.
2. Wilhelmina Barns-Graham, 'Collected Thoughts' in Douglas Hall (ed.), *W. Barns-Graham Retrospective: 1940–1989*, exh. cat. (Edinburgh: City of Edinburgh Museums and Art Galleries, 1989), p. 12. In 1989 Barns-Graham used the phrase 'lone wolf' to describe her modus operandi on arriving in St Ives in the 1940s, however, in later accounts she used the term with reference to distancing herself from the incestuous atmosphere of 'St Ives' in its heyday, see 'Wilhelmina Barns-Graham in conversation with Susan Loppert' in *Contemporary Art*, spring 1996, p. 20.
3. Douglas Hall, 'Introduction' in *W. Barns-Graham Retrospective: 1940–1989*, exh. cat. (Edinburgh: City of Edinburgh Museums and Art Galleries, 1989), p. 10.
4. 'Wilhelmina Barns-Graham: An Enduring Image', 1999, and 'Wilhelmina Barns-Graham: Movement and Light Imagin(in)ing Time', 2005.
5. Chris Stephens, *St Ives: The Art and the Artists* (London: Pavilion, Tate, 2018), p. 263 and pp. 127–29.
6. Quote by the artist in Loppert, Ibid., p. 20. Nedira Yakir has written about Barns-Graham from a feminist perspective in Katy Deepwell (ed.), *Women Artists and Modernism* (Manchester: Manchester University Press, 1998), pp. 112–28.
7. David Lewis, 'St Ives: A Personal Memoir, 1947–55' in David Brown (ed.), *St Ives, 1939–64: Twenty Five years of Painting, Sculpture and Pottery*, exh. cat. (London: Tate Gallery, 1985, new edition 1996), p. 25.
8. Loppert, Ibid., p. 20.
9. Michael Bird, *The St Ives Artists: A Biography of Place and Time* (London: Lund Humphries, 2008), p. 150.
10. Herbert Read, *The Meaning of Art* (London: Faber and Faber, 1931, revised 1972), p. 261.

11. Barns-Graham, 1989, Ibid., p. 12.
12. Barns-Graham underlined the following sentence in her 1951 copy of *The Meaning of Art*: 'The real function of art is to express *feeling* and transmit *understanding*', p. 189.
13. Herbert Read, *Art Now: An Introduction to the Theory of Modern Painting and Sculpture* (London: Faber and Faber, 1933, revised edition 1936), p. 155.
14. Wilhelmina Barns-Graham, 'Some Thoughts on Drawing' in *W. Barns-Graham Drawings*, exh. cat. (St Andrews: Crawford Art Centre, 1992) and Green, 2011, Ibid., p. 12.
15. Lynne Green, *Wilhelmina Barns-Graham: A Scottish Artist in St Ives* (Edinburgh: Wilhelmina Barns-Graham Trust, 2012, revised 2017).
16. For an explanation of synaesthesia see Chapter 4.

Life and Work

1. Douglas Hall, 'Introduction' in Douglas Hall (ed.), *W. Barns-Graham Retrospective: 1940–1989*, exh. cat. (Edinburgh: City of Edinburgh Museums and Art Galleries, 1989), p. 3.
2. 'Wilhelmina Barns-Graham in conversation with Susan Loppert', *Contemporary Art*, spring 1996, p. 20.
3. Hepworth wrote this in a letter to Barns-Graham prior to the 1950s. Nedira Yakir, 'Cornubia: gender, geography and genealogy in St Ives Modernism' in Katy Deepwell (ed.), *Women Artists and Modernism* (Manchester: Manchester University Press, 1998), p. 117. Hepworth was widely referred to as the 'Queen' of St Ives. Barns-Graham would have been aware of Hepworth's increasing resistance to gender-biased critique of her work, particularly in comparison with Henry Moore, as discussed by Deepwell, Ibid., pp. 97–111.

4. Wilhelmina Barns-Graham, 'Collected Thoughts' in Hall, Ibid., p. 12.

5. Lynne Green, *W. Barns-Graham: A Studio Life* (London: Lund Humphries, 2001, revised edition 2011), p. 27.

6. Loppert, Ibid., p. 18.

7. Green, 2011, Ibid., pp. 28–30.

8. Lynne Green, *Wilhelmina Barns-Graham: A Scottish Artist in St Ives* (Edinburgh: Wilhelmina Barns-Graham Trust, 2012, revised 2017), pp. 12–13.

9. Green, 2011, Ibid., pp. 36–40.

10. Green, 2011, Ibid., p. 56.

11. Borlase Smart cited in https://www.bsjwtrust.co.uk /artists/robert-borlase-smart/ [accessed 9 October 2019].

12. Mel Gooding, 'Wilhelmina Barns-Graham: a study in three movements' in Mel Gooding (ed.), *Wilhelmina Barns-Graham: Movement and Light Imag(in)ing Time*, exh. cat. (St Ives: Tate St Ives, 2005), pp. 10–11.

13. See Chris Stephens for an in depth account of the Crypt Group, in *St Ives: The Art and the Artists* (London: Pavilion and Tate, 2018), pp. 91–100, and specifically for Barns-Graham's involvement see Green, 2011, Ibid., pp. 89-94.

14. An established art historian and authority on modern art Read was instrumental in setting up London's Institute of Contemporary Art (ICA) and was on both Arts Council and British Council committees.

15. For details see David Brown (ed.), *St Ives, 1939–64: Twenty Five Years of Painting, Sculpture and Pottery*, exh. cat. (London: Tate Gallery, 1985, new edition 1996), pp. 106–9.

16. Green, 2011, Ibid., pp. 118–19.

17. Brown, Ibid., p. 162.

18. Barns-Graham in Hall, Ibid., p. 12.

19. See Green, 2011, Ibid., pp. 162–66, for a detailed account of the Golden Section and its use by Barns-Graham in the 1950s.

20. Loppert, Ibid., p. 20.

21. This followed her inclusion in a group show there in 1948, through an introduction to the gallery by Patrick Heron, then still based in London and making his name as art critic for the *New Statesman and Nation*, see Green, 2011, Ibid., p. 107 and p. 109.

22. Review in *Architectural Design*, vol. xxvi, July 1956, of her exhibition 'W. Barns-Graham: An Exhibition of Drawings from Scilly, Italy and South-west Cornwall' at the Scottish Gallery, Edinburgh, 7–28 July 1956.

23. Green, 2011, Ibid., p. 119.

24. Green, 2011, Ibid., p. 129.

25. Green, 2011, Ibid., pp. 160–61.

26. Green, 2011, Ibid., p. 166.

27. Green, 2011, Ibid., p. 166.

28. Stephens, Ibid., pp. 126–28.

29. Michael Bird, *The St Ives Artists: A Biography of Place and Time* (London: Lund Humphries, 2008) provides such a comment from William Gear to artist Sandra Blow, p. 150.

30. Green, 2011, Ibid., p. 139 and p. 144.

31. See Bird, Ibid., p. 148.

32. Nedira Yakir, 'W. Barns-Graham and Old Age: Celebration at 90' in Josephine Dolan and Estella Tincknell (eds.), *Ageing Femininities: Troubling Representations* (Cambridge: Cambridge Scholars Publishing, 2012), p. 39.

33. In her book *Barbara Hepworth: Carvings and Drawings* (London: Lund Humphries, 1952) Hepworth wrote: 'I have never understood why the word feminine is considered to be a compliment to one's sex if one is a woman, but has a derogatory meaning when applied to anything else.' Yakir, Ibid., pp. 123–24, has argued that abstraction allowed Barns-Graham and other women artists to evade gender categorisation.

34. Margaret Garlake, *New Art New World: British Art in Postwar Society* (New Haven: Yale University Press, 1998), pp. 102–3.

35. Hall, Ibid., p. 10.

36. She read Jung, Adler, Kant, Ouspensky and Gurdjieff and flirted with Christian Science and the Baha'i faith, finally committing to the Anglican Church through confirmation in May 1965. Green, 2011, Ibid., pp. 192–93.

37. Green, 2011, Ibid., p. 170.

38. Terry Frost was taught by Pasmore at Camberwell School of Art, and introduced him to the Nicholson-Hepworth circle and St Ives. Pasmore was elected to the Penwith Society in January 1951.

39. Victor Pasmore, statement at the ICA, London on 9 January 1951, later published in *Art News & Review*. See Alastair Grieve, *Constructed Abstract Art in England: A Neglected Avant-garde* (New Haven: Yale University Press, 2005), p. 75.

40. Green, 2011, Ibid., p. 167.

41. Barns-Graham in Hall, Ibid., p. 13.

42. Geoffrey Bertram, *Wilhelmina Barns-Graham: A Journey Through Four Decades*, exh. cat. (Edinburgh: The Scottish Gallery, 2019), p. 16.

43. Barns-Graham in Hall, Ibid., p. 13.

44. Barns-Graham reported that although she drew in front of the motif, she also turned her back on the sea to draw its movements from memory. See 'Wilhelmina Barns-Graham interviewed by Tamsin Woollcombe in *National Life Stories: Artists' Lives* (London: The British Library, 1994), https:sounds.bl.uk [accessed 13 May 2019].

45. Barns-Graham identified with the idea of the 'looking in-looking out' kind of artist, as described by her artist friend Winifred Nicholson (1893–1981) in Hall, Ibid., p. 12.

46. Artist's statement in *Freeing the Spirit: Contemporary Scottish Abstraction*, exh. cat. (St Andrews: Crawford Centre for the Arts, 1988).

47. The artist's synaesthesia and its impact on her work are discussed in more detail in Chapter 4.

48. Hall, Ibid., p. 11; Barns-Graham in Hall, Ibid., p. 13.

49. Ann Gunn, *The Prints of Wilhelmina Barns-Graham: A Complete Catalogue* (London: Lund Humphries, 2007), p. 53.

50. Picasso in *Cahiers d'Art*, vol. X, 1935, at p. 174, quoted by Herbert Read in *Art Now: An Introduction to the Theory of Modern Painting and Sculpture* (London: Faber and Faber 1933, revised 1936), p. 147.

Abstraction

1. The artist quoted by J.P. Hodin, 'Cornish Renaissance' in John Lehmann (ed.), *Penguin New Writing*, no. 39 (London: Penguin, 1950).

2. Lynne Green, *W. Barns-Graham: A Studio Life* (London: Lund Humphries, 2001, revised 2011), p. 119.

3. Michael Bird, *The St Ives Artists: A Biography of Place and Time* (London: Lund Humphries, 2008), p. 148.

4. Virginia Button, *Ben Nicholson* (London: Tate, 2007), pp. 58–59.

5. Chris Stephens, *St Ives: The Art and the Artists* (London: Pavilion and Tate, 2018), p. 61.

6. She was acquainted with Thompson as a child – the Chair of Natural History at St Andrews University from 1917 until his death in 1948 he was a well-known local figure in her home town – though it's unlikely she read his theories before the early 1940s.

7. See Herbert Read, *Art and Society* (London: Faber and Faber, revised edition 1945), p. 125 and 'Realism and Abstraction in Modern Art' in *The Philosophy of Modern Art* (London: Faber and Faber, 1952).

8. Stephens, Ibid., pp. 133–34. Thompson's theories permeated art circles at this time, for example, in 1951 his seminal text provided the pretext for the ICA's exhibition 'Growth and Form', organised by Richard Hamilton (1922–2011).

9. Barns-Graham, letter to Allan and Wilhelmina Menzies Barns-Graham, 1 June 1947, University of St Andrews Special Collections.

10. Green, Ibid., p. 107.

11. *The Tate Gallery Report 1964–65* (HMSO1966) (London: Tate, 1966), p. 30.

12. Like Barns-Graham, Lanyon, Wells and Wynter were also interested in Gabo's treatment of form and space, and his motif of an encased centre. His wartime paintings investigating the articulation of constructions, and use of colour demonstrated how the constructivist idea could be applied in two dimensions. For discussion of Gabo's influence on the younger 'St Ives' artists see Stephens, Ibid., pp. 55–57.

13. Herbert Read, 'Constructivism: The Art of Naum Gabo and Antoine Pevsner' in *Gabo-Pevsner*, exh. cat. (New York: Museum of Modern Art, 1948), p. 11.

14. Mel Gooding, 'Wilhelmina Barns-Graham: a study in three movements' in Mel Gooding (ed.), *Wilhelmina Barns-Graham: Movement and Light Imag(in)ing Time* exh. cat. (St Ives: Tate St Ives, 2005), p. 13.

15. Jaquetta Hawkes, *A Land* (London: The Cresset Press, 1951), p. 1. The book was illustrated with drawings by Moore and Nicholson.

16. Patrick Elliott, *The Two Roberts: Robert Colquhoun & Robert MacBryde* (Edinburgh: National Galleries of Scotland, 2014), pp. 86–87.

17. Ann Gunn, *The Prints of Wilhelmina Barns-Graham: A Complete Catalogue* (London: Lund Humphries, 2007), p. 15.

18. Quoted by Green, Ibid, p. 119.

19. Barns-Graham's notes to J.P. Hodin about her work dated 1948 though they were most likely written in 1949. See Green, Ibid., p. 316, fn. 21.

20. Barns-Graham quoted by J.P. Hodin, Ibid.,
and quote from Barns-Graham's notes to Hodin.
21. Rachel Rose Smith, 'A new involvement in form:
Barns-Graham, Switzerland and Italy' in *Wilhelmina
Barns-Graham: Inspirational Journeys* (Edinburgh:
Wilhelmina Barns-Graham Trust, 2019), p. 15.
22. Green, Ibid., p. 137.
23. Hodin, Ibid.
24. Herbert Read, *The Meaning of Art* (London:
Faber and Faber, 1931, revised 1951), pp. 83–84.

Drawing

1. 'Wilhelmina Barns-Graham in conversation with
Susan Loppert', *Contemporary Art*, spring 1996, p. 20.
2. Mel Gooding, 'Wilhelmina Barns-Graham: a study
in three movements' in Mel Gooding (ed.), *Wilhelmina
Barns-Graham: Movement and Light Imag(in)ing Time*,
exh. cat. (London: Tate, 2005), p. 12.
3. Tania Kovats (ed.), *The Drawing Book A Survey of
Drawing: The Primary Means of Expression* (London:
Black Dog Publishing, 2007), p. 9.
4. 'Wilhelmina Barns-Graham interviewed by Tamsin
Woollcombe' in *National Life Stories: Artists' Lives*
(London: The British Library, 1994) https://sounds.bl.uk
[accessed on 13 May 2019].
5. Lynne Green, *Wilhelmina Barns-Graham: A Scottish
Artist in St Ives* (Edinburgh: Wilhelmina Barns-Graham
Trust, 2012, revised 2017), p. 12.
6. Wilhelmina Barns-Graham, 'Some Thoughts on
Drawing' in *W. Barns-Graham: Drawings*, exh. cat.
(St Andrews: Crawford Art Centre, 1992).
7. Martin Kemp, 'Fateful Lines: Drawings by W. Barns-
Graham' in *W. Barns-Graham Drawings*, exh. cat.
(St Andrews: Crawford Art Centre, 1992).
8. Barns-Graham, Ibid.
9. Barns-Graham, Ibid. Her use of the phrase 'the
essence of things', most likely refers to a statement
by Constantin Brancusi, who she admired: 'They are
imbeciles who call my work abstract; that which they
call abstract is the most realistic, because what is
real is not the exterior form but the idea, the essence
of things.' Claire Gilles Guibert, 'Propos de Brancusi'
in *Prisme des Arts*, no. 12, May 1957, translated and
reproduced in Herschel B. Chipp, *Theories of Modern
Art: A Source Book by Artists and Critics* (Berkeley:
University of California Press, 1968), p. 365.
10. Mel Gooding, *A Discipline of the Mind: The Drawings
of Wilhelmina Barns-Graham*, exh. cat. (Stromness and
Edinburgh: The Pier Arts Centre and Barns-Graham
Charitable Trust, 2009), p. 7.
11. Barns-Graham, Ibid.
12. Quotations from the English translation by
Norbert Guterman in Paul Klee (ed.), *The Inward
Vision; watercolours, drawings, writings* (New York:
Abrams, 1959), reprinted in Chipp, Ibid., p. 183.

13. Denys Val Baker, *Britain's Art Colony by the Sea*
(Welwyn: George Ronald, 1959), p. 47.
14. David Lewis letter to Krister Lagergren,
27 September 1954, WBG TA (Wilhelmina Barnes-
Graham Archive). Quoted in Green, Ibid., p. 150.
15. Lynne Green discusses Barns-Graham's anxiety
about Nicholson also making works in Chiusure,
following his purchase of one of her drawings, as
she felt critical opinion would assume she had been
influenced by him, see Lynne Green, *W. Barns-Graham:
A Studio Life* (London: Lund Humphries, 2001, revised
2011), p. 155.
16. Barns-Graham, Ibid.
17. The artist quoted in Rob Airey 'Orkney' in
Wilhelmina Barns-Graham: Inspirational Journeys
(Edinburgh: Wilhelmina Barns-Graham Trust, 2019),
p. 51.
18. 'A Distant Isle: Wilhelmina Barns-Graham in
Lanzarote' in *Wilhelmina Barns-Graham Trust: Abstract*,
issue 6, June 2019, https://www.barns-grahamtrust.
org.uk [accessed 4 July 2019].
19. Lanyon died in 1964, Hepworth, Hilton and Wynter
in 1975, followed by Nicholson in 1982.
20. Barns-Graham, Ibid.
21. Barns-Graham, Ibid.

Colour

1. The artist identified with 'the looking in-looking
out' kind of artist described by her friend Winifred
Nicholson, see Wilhelmina Barns-Graham, 'Collected
Thoughts' in Douglas Hall (ed.), *W. Barns-Graham
Retrospective: 1940–1989*, exh. cat. (Edinburgh: City
of Edinburgh Museums and Art Galleries, 1989), p. 12.
2. 'Kasimir Malevich (1878–1935) "Non-Objective Art
and Suprematism"', in Charles Harrison and Paul Wood
(eds.), *Art in Theory 1900–1990: An Anthology of
Changing Ideas* (Bew Jersey: Blackwell, 1992), p. 291.
3. Lynne Green quotes Barns-Graham's note in full
in *W. Barns-Graham: A Studio Life* (London: Lund
Humphries, 2001, revised 2011), p. 300.
4. Wilhelmina Barns-Graham quoted in John McEwen
'A Painter on the Edge of Urgency' in *Sunday Telegraph*,
25 March 2001.
5. Wilhelmina Barns-Graham, 'Artist's Statement:
Wilhelmina Barns-Graham' in Penny Florence and
Nicola Foster (eds.), *Differential Aesthetics. Art Practices,
Philosophy and Feminist Understandings* (Farnham:
Ashgate, 2000), p. 29.
6. The artist, quoted by Lynne Green in *Looking in
Looking out – A Film on Wilhelmina Barns-Graham* by
Tim Fitzpatrick (2012) https://www.barns-grahamtrust.
org.uk/The-Trust/articles/Article-7.html [accessed
4 November 2019]. It is worth noting that scientific
interest in synaesthesia diminished between the
1940s and 1980s.

7. Jane Beckett, 'Introduction' in *Wilhelmina Barns-Graham 1912–2004: A Tribute: Recent Paintings & New Prints*, exh. cat. (London: Art First, 2004), p. 11.

8. Barns-Graham in Hall, Ibid., p.13, quotes Psalm 100: 'Come before His presence with a song'. The idea of singing through her paintings also points to her synesthetic experience.

9. Green, Ibid., p. 16.

10. Robert Adam, 'Willie Barns-Graham — A personal appreciation' in *Wilhelmina Barns-Graham 1912–2004*, exh. cat. (London: Art First, 2004), pp. 39–43.

11. Lynne Green, *Wilhelmina Barns-Graham: A Scottish Artist in St Ives* (Edinburgh: Wilhelmina Barns-Graham Trust, 2012, revised 2017), p. 13.

12. Philip Long, *The Scottish Colourists 1900–1930* (Edinburgh: National Galleries of Scotland, 2000), p. 13.

13. Wilhelmina Barns-Graham, 'October 1980', *Art Monthly*, July/August 1981, p. 5.

14. Quoted by Rachel Rose Smith in 'A new involvement in form: Barns-Graham, Switzerland and Italy' in *Wilhelmina Barns-Graham: Inspirational Journeys* (Edinburgh: Wilhelmina Barns-Graham Trust, 2019), p. 19. The artist visited Italy in summer 1950 and purchased a book on Piero della Francesca on her return to St Ives.

15. Michael Williams, 'W. Barns-Graham' in *Cornish Magazine*, vol. 4, no. 10, February 1962.

16. Frederick A. Horowitz and Brenda Danilowitz, *Josef Albers: To Open Eyes* (London: Phaidon, 2006, paperback 2009), p. 200.

17. Horowitz and Danilowitz, Ibid., p. 198. Hilton, who settled in Cornwall in 1965, also explored this active potential of colour.

18. Green, 2011, Ibid., p.193.

19. Michel Leiris, 'A Genius without a Pedestal' in *Late Picasso: Paintings, Sculpture, Drawings, Prints 1953–1972*, exh. cat. (London: The Tate Gallery, 1988), p. 15.

20. See Rob Airey, 'Orkney' in *Wilhelmina Barns-Graham: Inspirational Journeys* (Edinburgh: Wilhelmina Barns-Graham Trust, 2019), p. 51.

21. Green, 2011, Ibid., pp. 268–69.

22. Ann Gunn, *The Prints of Wilhelmina Barns-Graham: A Complete Catalogue* (London: Lund Humphries, 2007), p. 52.

23. Green, 2011, Ibid., p. 269.

24. Gunn, Ibid., p. 56.

25. The artist quoted by Green, 2011, Ibid., p. 260.

26. Kassia St Clair, *The Secret Lives of Colour* (London: John Murray, 2016), p. 179 and p. 182.

27. Barns-Graham in Hall, Ibid. p. 12.

Acknowledgements

I would like to thank all those who have generously assisted me in writing this book, especially Professor Alan Livingston CBE, former Principal of Falmouth University and others in the art community in Cornwall who have shared their memories of the artist, who remains an important figure in St Ives. I'm particularly grateful to the Wilhelmina Barns-Graham Trust (WBGT) for inviting me to reassess the life and work of this pioneering British woman artist. As former Director of Falmouth School of Art at Falmouth University in Cornwall, I greatly appreciated the ongoing commitment of the Trust (and 'Willie') to supporting young artists through a series of bursaries and travelling scholarships. This is an important aspect of the artist's legacy I've not touched on in this book, but it was typical of Willie to reflect on her own positive experiences and, understanding the challenges of pursuing an artist's life, to want others to benefit from opportunities as she had done. As a Tate curator, in the early 1990s I visited her studio in St Ives with a group of Tate's patrons. Willie struck me then as young in spirit, and despite her achievements and reputation for being direct and outspoken she was modest, preferring the work to do its magic, rather than trying to impress her guests.

I'm hugely indebted to Lynne Green's primary research, particularly her definitive monograph *W. Barns-Graham: A Studio Life* (2001, revised 2011) published with the artist's approval and to the deep knowledge of Willie's advocate in her later decades, Geoffrey Bertram. The WBGT archive in Edinburgh is an extraordinary repository of the artist's work across her career and I'd like especially to thank the Trust's Director, Rob Airey, and former Collections Manager, Ross Irving, for giving me access to its holdings and for sharing their invaluable insights. The scope of this book means that it has been impossible to cover every aspect of the phenomenal volume and diversity of Barns-Graham's output, but I hope that it will prompt further curiosity and research.

Much gratitude to all the public and private collections who have supplied images of Barns-Grahams in their collections and given permission to reproduce them and also many thanks to the copyright-holders for works by Naum Gabo, Barbara Hepworth and Ben Nicholson for allowing them to be reproduced in this book.

Finally, I'd like to thank the staff at Sansom & Co. for their support in realising this handsome book, and to my husband Tom Scott and daughters Marina and Clem, for their encouragement throughout.

Virginia Button

Index